303.625   Emerson, Steven.
EME
          American Jihad.

$26.00

DATE			

DO NOT REMOVE
Date Due Card

Also by Steven Emerson

Terrorist: The Inside Story of the Highest-Ranking
Iraqi Terrorist Ever to Defect to the West *(with Cristina del Sesto)*

The Fall of Pan Am 103 *(with Brian Duffy)*

Secret Warriors: Inside the Covert Military Operations
of the Reagan Era

The American House of Saud:
The Secret Petrodollar Connection

AMERICAN
JIHAD

THE TERRORISTS
LIVING AMONG US

STEVEN EMERSON

THE FREE PRESS

New York London Toronto Sydney Singapore

THE FREE PRESS
A Division of Simon & Schuster, Inc.
1230 Avenue of the Americas
New York, NY 10020

Manufactured in the United States of America

10   9   8   7   6   5   4   3   2   1

Library of Congress Cataloging-in-Publication Data is available.

ISBN 0-7432-3324-7

For information regarding special discounts for bulk purchases,
please contact Simon & Schuster Special Sales at 1-800-456-6798 or
business@simonandschuster.com

Contents

The Jihad, the fighting, is obligatory on you wherever you can perform it. And just as when you are in America you must fast—unless you are ill or on a voyage—so, too, must you wage Jihad. The word Jihad means fighting only, fighting with the sword.

—Abdullah Azzam
Oklahoma City, 1988

"TAKE UP ARMS AND ARMS ALONE!"

THE VEILED COMMANDER STOOD UP, a Hamas flag in one hand and a Koran in the other. The crowd roared "Allahu akbar walillahi'l-hamd!" ("Allah is great and to Allah we give praise!")—the slogan of the international Muslim Brotherhood movement. This was the moment everyone seemed to have been waiting for.

His face still veiled in a red-and-white checkered *keffiyeh*, the Hamas commander spoke: "Greetings . . . from the occupied land . . . I extend thanks to all those who stood on our side at times when our allies were few." He gave a report describing in methodical detail Hamas terrorist attacks, reveling in the bloody results of each assault: "Naturally the war has moved into Israel's '48 boundaries. One day in Tel Aviv, one of the brothers entered a building and began stabbing all the people. . . . The last operation I am going to tell you about is the operation of the bus—"

The anticipation was too great—shouts of "Allahu akbar!" erupted from the crowd, which sensed exactly what he was going to discuss. "[One of our fighters] was on the bus to Jerusalem, Bus 405 and he steered it off the road. . . . And the bus plunged . . . sixteen Jewish soldiers were killed!" In fact, seventeen civilians, including one American, were killed when a fundamentalist steered this particular bus into a ravine. ". . . I call upon my brothers to take up arms with us . . . to take up arms and arms alone!" The crowd responded with a thunderous ovation and chanting of "Allahu akbar!"

The date: 1989. The location: Kansas City. The commander was addressing and thanking the Islamic Association for Palestine and the Occupied Land Fund, two organizations holding a conference in the country they called home.

The dream of a world under Islam has engendered Muslim dissidents everywhere in the world over the last two decades. Almost every Islamic country has its militant faction, often two or three. The Hamas of Palestine, Hizballah of Iran, the Islamic Salvation Front and Armed Islamic Group of Algeria, An-Nahda of Tunisia, the Muslim Brotherhood and al-Gamaʿat al-Islamiyya of Egypt, the Jamaʿat Muslimeen of Pakistan, and the Holy Warriors of the Philippines and Chechnya—all share the same goal of an Islamic world, or, as they refer to it, a *Khilafah*.

In the past twelve years, however, these groups have achieved a new level of coordination, owing to their exploitation of the civil liberties of the United States. None of these small national groups was ever able to coordinate its worldwide efforts with the others until they came to the United States. Operating in our open society, with freedom of speech and assembly and with only casual oversight from the FBI, the CIA, and the Immigration and Naturalization Service, the worldwide network of militant Islamic organizations has finally been able to coordinate. They have operated here both in order to direct activities in the Middle East, and to target America. The attacks on the World Trade Center and the Pentagon on September 11, 2001, were only part of the results.

After September 11, 2001, everyone in America knows full well the power and persistence of these militant radical groups. It is a certainty that terrorists, already living among us, will continue to pursue their destructive agenda. Whether they succeed may depend in part upon whether we can recognize how they operate. This book offers a twelve-year-long story of the arrival and flourishing of terrorists in the United States, explaining where they are, how they interconnect, how they recruit, how they raise money, and how they use our legal system as a cover.

Call it jihad, American style—or the American Jihad.

Chapter One

HOW I MADE "JIHAD IN AMERICA" AND LIVED TO TELL ABOUT IT

IN DECEMBER 1992 I was a staff reporter for CNN, covering what I consider one of the worst stories imaginable—a press conference for pool reporters.

In this case the conference was given by Lawrence Walsh, the former special prosecutor for the Iran-*contra* affair, who was issuing a statement in reaction to then-President George Bush's pardon of former secretary of state Caspar Weinberger. It was the kind of situation where more than a dozen reporters ask the same question over and over, then go back and write the same story.

In short, I was bored. In Oklahoma City, I found myself with nothing to do on Christmas Day. As I walked around looking for a place to eat, I passed a large group of men dressed in traditional Middle Eastern clothing.

These men had congregated outside of the Oklahoma City Convention Center. I realized there was some kind of convention going on. Drawn to the scene, I wandered inside and found a bazaar of vendors hawking all kinds of radical material. There were books preaching Islamic "Jihad," books calling for the extermination of Jews and Christians, even coloring books instructing children on subjects such as "How to Kill the Infidel." It was a meeting of the Muslim Arab Youth Association (MAYA), an umbrella group that included many smaller groups.

When I asked admittance to the main meeting hall, I was told that as a non-Muslim I couldn't enter. But I found my way into a group of "recent converts," where I was befriended by a man who sponsored my admission. I ended up sitting through the entire program. It was a shocking experience. Given simultaneous translation by a jihadist next to me, I was horrified to witness a long procession of speakers, including the head of Hamas, Khalid Misha'al, taking turns preaching violence and urging the assembly to use jihad against the Jews and the West. At times spontaneous shouts of "Kill the Jews" and "Destroy the West" could be distinctly heard. I had heard such declamatory speakers many times in the Middle East, but it was astonishing to hear it all being preached here in a Middle American capital such as Oklahoma City.

I had some contacts in the FBI at this point and called one to see if he knew that all of this was going on. He said he didn't. Even if the FBI had been cognizant, however, there wouldn't have been much they could do about it, owing to the FBI's mandate to surveil criminal activity and not simply hateful rhetoric.

Just how far behind the FBI had fallen in keeping abreast of these potentially dangerous subversive groups became clear a year later when I attended a five-day Muslim conference in Detroit in December 1993. This annual gathering featured speakers and representatives from some of the world's most militant fundamentalist organizations, including Hamas, the Muslim Brotherhood, Palestinian Islamic Jihad, and many others. After five days of listening to speakers urging Muslims to wage jihad, I was startled to hear that a senior FBI agent from the Detroit office would be making an unscheduled appearance on the program. Sure enough, the official showed up. After making some perfunctory remarks about civil rights, the official asked for questions from the visibly hostile audience. A series of scornful responses followed, including that of one audience member who asked, tongue in cheek, if the agent could give the group any advice on "shipping weapons" overseas to their friends. The FBI official said matter-of-factly that he hoped any such efforts would be done in conformance with the Bureau of Alcohol, Tobacco, and Firearms guidelines.

Returning to Washington again, I asked FBI officials if they knew that their Detroit colleague had spoken at this radical gathering. They assured me it was impossible. After checking, however, they admitted within a few hours that their man had indeed been there, mistakenly thinking it was "some kind of Rotary Club."

I soon learned that the FBI could do little or nothing to monitor such groups. Congressional restrictions imposed following disclosure in the 1970s of abuses by law enforcement and intelligence agencies had long since prevented the FBI from performing "blanket surveillance." Investigations could only be done on particular individuals and then only if these individuals appeared to be in the act of committing a crime. Regulations, as former FBI official Oliver Revell has stated, forbade them from compiling even "open source" information—articles that appear in the newspaper, for instance—without receiving prior permission to open up an "investigation." Indeed, individual FBI investigators could be personally sued for engaging in surveillance activities that went beyond these guidelines. Several agents had been the targets of such lawsuits and most FBI agents had become extremely wary of straying outside the lines. Even more significant, the FBI was particularly hamstrung if these groups operated under the auspices of "religious," "civic," "civil rights," or "charitable" groups. This has provided cover for recruiting and fundraising by jihad warriors in the United States.

*   *   *

I was still working for CNN in 1993 when the first World Trade Center bombing occurred on February 26th. As the story unfolded it became obvious that the whole plot had been hatched among small terror cells in this country. I had heard an excess of explosive rhetoric in Oklahoma City and other places where I had investigated militant organizations. I was sure there must be some connection.

But I was faced with a difficult moral dilemma. I hadn't started investigating anyone to any great degree. All I had at that point was a collection of books and pamphlets and promotional material by which these groups advertised themselves to a very select audience. I didn't know whether it was all rhetoric or whether there was really substance to all this. I had a few videos showing that Hamas had definitely established itself in this country, but that was about it. Would I be risking my career by following up this story, in what might prove to be a wild goose chase?

I decided to take a proposal to Richard Carlson of the Corporation for Public Broadcasting. Already I was thinking in terms of a video. I'm a print journalist by background but here was a story that would be much easier to tell as a TV program. The most dramatic material I was collecting was already in video form anyway. The training and recruitment videos, the fiery speeches at mosques and conventions—it would be hard to convey the blood-curdling nature of this material except by letting it speak for itself.

Carlson liked the idea and passed it up the line. Before long I was passed over to the Public Broadcasting System, the network subsidiary of CPB. I ended up dealing with Bob Coonrod and Ervin Duggan, who was then president of PBS. They were very enthusiastic but couldn't generate much interest within the bureaucracy of PBS. Finally, Dugin took matters into his own hands and provided me with some research and development money.

And so in 1993 I left CNN to work full-time as an investigator of terrorist networks in the United States. I founded The Investigative Project, which has employed a shifting staff of from two to fifteen people. What we discovered is that, indeed, international terrorist organizations of all sorts had set up shop here in America. They often took advantage of religious, civic, or charitable organizations. Usually this was more than enough to fool the public, the police, and especially naive leaders of religious or educational institutions, who were more than willing to encourage and sponsor these groups in the name of "multiculturalism" and "diversity." Meanwhile, U.S.-based terrorists have been able to use these organizations to ferry equipment to Middle Eastern terror groups, to offer financial support to the families of suicide bombers, to coordinate efforts with other terrorist networks around the world, and ultimately to plan and support terrorist acts in the United States.

It took us a while to piece all this together. Going to conferences and collecting promotional material had its limits. We could attend mosque services, but much of them was in Arabic. Early on, I hooked up with a friend named Khalid Duran, and he began providing translation services for much of the written and video material. But it was slow going.

Then one day I found myself standing in a Yemeni grocery store in Brooklyn. I looked around and spotted dozens of copies of dusty videos that appeared to have something to do with commandos and rifles. I bought twenty different tapes—much to the astonishment of the store owner. When I got them into Khalid's hands we realized we were looking at paramilitary training videos for the leaders of Islamic militant groups. One of them was put out by an organization called the Islamic Association for Palestine, in Richardson, Texas. To our horror, it showed the actual torment and forced "confessions" of Palestinian "collaborators" moments before they were executed.

We followed up this material by traveling to Texas, Florida, and New York to try to arrange interviews with the leaders of these groups. For the most part they were not very cooperative. We got very little footage. Slowly, however, we were beginning to accumulate enough material to put together a documentary.

Part of the task, I realized, would be tracing some of these organizations to their origins in the Middle East and beyond. I started in Israel. I had learned by this time that the first calls for worldwide jihad had come from Abdullah Azzam, the Palestinian mullah who had set up a waystation in Peshawar, Pakistan for Muslim recruits who wanted to take part in the jihad against the Soviet Union in Afghanistan. One afternoon, riding around the West Bank in a taxicab, I was talking absentmindedly with my Palestinian driver when I mentioned Azzam. "Oh, his brother-in-law lives here just north of here," the driver said. He gave me the name of the village of Jenin.

The next day I found another driver and headed for Jenin. All I had was Azzam's name and the name of the village. When we got there and asked a few people, however, they quickly directed us to his house. Azzam was very gracious and immediately welcomed me in. He told me about his experience in Peshawar and about his brother-in-law. It was a strange encounter. At the time, Palestinian electricity was not very reliable and every ten minutes or so the lights would go out, plunging us into total darkness.

Azzam told me he had other relatives living in Chicago. When I got back to the United States, I called them up and arranged to visit one of Azzam's nephews. Khalid came with me. We rendezvoused at a small Middle Eastern restaurant in Bridgeview, Illinois, a suburb southwest of Chicago. The nephew was very gracious. He was not aware that I was collecting information and I didn't make any attempt to misrepresent myself. I simply said I was interested in his family and anxious to write about them. He told me about Hudaifah, one of Abdullah's sons, and said he was trying to hold together his father's organization in Peshawar.

Later he took Khalid and me to the Bridgeview Mosque, where Jamal Said was the imam. I could tell immediately that we were deep in the heart of Hamas territory. The walls of the vestibule were covered with Hamas posters and recruiting literature showing masked gunmen brandishing automatic weapons. It was all in Arabic, but you could see daggers plunged into Jewish hearts wrapped up in American flags. They even had a library filled with militant terrorist videos and books. Khalid was there to translate for me. The Friday service was a rather strange experience. Out of eight hundred people, I was the only one wearing a red ski jacket. When the service was over I approached the imam and asked him if he had known Abdullah Azzam. He was very defensive. "I never met with him," he said quickly and then dismissed me. Earlier that year, two Hamas operatives, congregants of the mosque, were arrested in Israel for transferring money from the United States to terrorists on the West Bank. One of these men, Mohammad Jarad, told the Israelis that he was sent on his mission by Jamal Said.

*　　*　　*

"Jihad in America" was broadcast on November 21, 1994. It showed in the 10:00 P.M. slot on a Thursday night. Militant Islamic groups began to protest even before the show was aired. Several weeks before the showing, the Council on American-Islamic Relations (CAIR) issued a press release that a mosque in Brooklyn had been set on fire. The sub-title: "PBS 'Jihad in America' documentary may prompt more hate crimes." The implication, of course, was that the violent backlash against Muslims—even a month before the film was to air—had already begun. (When police investigated the fire, they found that it had been set on a rug in an upstairs apartment—over an internal dispute.)

"Jihad in America" pulled together a fair representation of the material we had collected. We showed Hamas operatives and militant mullahs preaching jihad and violence "with the gun" against Israel and America. We didn't show the torture and confessions of Palestinian collaborators—that would have been too inflammatory. The documentary continuously stressed the fact that militant Islamists are only a minute percentage of the Muslim population. Nevertheless, the film was attacked, and I was called a "crusader," a "racist," and just about everything else. To say it was disconcerting would be an understatement. I never anticipated the degree to which these groups were going to try to deny what was going on. They claimed that I was making it all up and that I had fabricated the tapes. I was also amazed at how far some prominent mainstream newspapers would do the same, some running several highly skeptical and critical editorials. Other newspapers simply used the tried-and-true method of being "even-handed." On the one hand, Steve Emerson says militant Islamic groups are bringing jihad to America. On the other hand, Islamic groups deny it.

Despite all the skepticism, the fights, and the controversy, "Jihad in America" won the prestigious George Polk Award. It was also named the "best investigative reporting in print, broadcast or book" by the Investigative Reporters and Editors Organization. It won the National Headliner Award and the Chris Award as well.

Suddenly thrust into the public eye, I encountered situations I had never dealt with before. One night I was taking a cab back to my apartment from Reagan National Airport in Washington. I glanced at the front seat and saw an Arabic-language newspaper. On the front page was my picture with a bull's-eye superimposed on it. I realized my life was going to be very different from then on.

Once I found myself at a Muslim convention where a speaker started shouting, "Steven Emerson is the enemy of Islam! Are we going to let Steven Emerson tell us what to do?" "No," the crowd roared in response. I sat there sweating. Thankfully, I had altered my appearance. Even so, I was exceptionally nervous. Fortunately, no one noticed me.

Over the years The Investigative Project's acquisition of materials has become quite sophisticated. We subscribe to more than a hundred radical periodicals a month and acquire hundreds more documents from sources, conventions, rallies, and other venues. We sustain a rigorous effort to collect video- and audio-tapes of radical Islamic groups and leaders in action. We have translators working full-time, and often send Arabic-speaking representatives to conventions and other gatherings, since this is the only way to understand fully what is going on. We have logged more than 6,000 hours of video- and audiotapes and our electronic library is probably the most comprehensive in the world. We have compiled a database of some thousands of individuals who are known or suspected terrorists, or direct supporters of terrorists, as well as dossiers on scores of militant groups.

The Investigative Project built on its own momentum. We became a collection point. People started calling up and asking, "What do you know?" or "Do you know this?" We received countless tips. Most of them turned out to be bogus, but a few were incredibly fruitful.

Then the death threats began. It started in South Africa. A public television station in that country announced it was going to show "Jihad in America." Radical Islamic groups immediately went to court and tried to block it. Much to our satisfaction, a South African court ruled in our favor. The show ran, with a good deal of pre-publicity.

A short time later I got an urgent call from the U.S. law enforcement officials. I was working in my Washington apartment. They told me to get in a taxi and come downtown immediately, making sure no one was following me. They gave me an address in Foggy Bottom. When I got there it turned out to be the offices of the Bureau of Diplomatic Security (BDS), an arm of the State Department that deals largely with terrorism.

FBI and BDS officials quickly briefed me. After "Jihad in America" aired in South Africa, a militant Muslim group had taken offense. They had dispatched a team to assassinate me. The State Department and FBI had only found out recently; as far as they knew, which unfortunately was not a lot, the assassins had already entered the country. It was even possible they already had me under surveillance. The problem was that the FBI simply had no idea whether or not the militants had entered the country.

"What would you like to do?" they asked me.

"What can I do?" I asked.

Well, there wasn't too much. One thing that was out of the question was round-the-clock police protection. That was too expensive. I was only a private citizen and it wasn't in anybody's budget. They would send a team of officers out to my apartment to discuss the options.

The next day a whole team came to my Connecticut Avenue condominium—FBI officials, federal counterterrorism experts, detectives from both the District of Columbia and Metropolitan Police Departments—the latter being the guards of the Capitol area.

Here were the possibilities:

- "You can stop what you're doing, don't write about it anymore, don't say anything, don't appear on television, and maybe after a while people will just forget about it."

- "We can see if the federal witness protection program can handle you. This will mean moving to a different city and assuming a new identity."

- "Maybe we can put you up in New York in a safe house for about a year. After that, you're on your own."

I was amazed. For years I had thought of myself as an observer, taking note of events, writing down notes, making reports, storing information for future reference. Now I was an active participant in one of my stories, and I wasn't sure that I liked it.

I told them none of this sounded very appealing. I would think it over. Meanwhile, I was given one prop. They presented me with a collapsible mirror that I could carry around with me and use every time I got into my car to check to make sure a car bomb had not been attached to the underside of the engine. As any rational person would do under the circumstances, I used it quite a bit.

After thinking it over for a day or so, I made up my mind. I wasn't going to give up investigating. I wasn't going to move to New York. I wasn't going to assume a new identity. But I would have to move out of my apartment and live underground for a while. This was not an easy decision. I had bought my condominium six years before—the first time I had owned my own home. I couldn't buy anything new. It would take too long to sell the old one and I might have to be moving regularly anyway. I had to develop new habits. The D.C. Police Department parked a cruiser outside my house for fifteen hours a day while I was making arrangements. Even then I had to sleep somewhere else to be safe. I had about a week before I was on my own again.

The police taught me some techniques about living underground. Stay away from the windows. Vary your routine. The important thing is not to leave the house at the same time or take the same route to and from the office every day. When driving a car, make sure no one is following you. Do a quick U-turn every once in a while just to make sure. I did that many times.

"Be careful when you jog," they said. That was a big problem. I love to jog. It's my only opportunity to get outdoors and get my mind off things for a while. But jogging through Rock Creek Park at night promised maximum exposure. Now I had to develop a hundred different ways of leaving my apartment and winding through different streets in inconspicuous clothing in order to

maintain my daily exercise. If I didn't my health—and sanity—
would probably collapse. It was trying and unnerving.

Along the way I had to decide whether this was all worth it.
Did I really want to live this way? Couldn't I just move on to another subject and be just as effective as an investigator and reporter? I weighed the idea for a long time. But there was a stubborn
resistance in me. I didn't like the idea of being intimidated. I'd be
giving up an extremely good story. I honestly believed this was an
important concern for everyone in the nation. I could see the momentum toward domestic terror building. I decided to go on.

One incident that severely affected the course of my reporting
was the Oklahoma City bombing of April 1995. That ended up
being an albatross around my neck. Less than six hours after the
bombing I was asked on television whether I thought militant Islamic groups were involved. There was good reason for thinking
they might be. The bombing, after all, was in Oklahoma City, where
I had first encountered such militant groups in 1992. Several Hamas
operatives were known to be living in the Oklahoma City area. At
first federal law-enforcement officials were suspicious themselves.

When asked on a news program, I responded that "federal
law enforcement officials" were investigating the possibility that
militant Islamic groups were involved. This was true. I also said
that "this [was] done with the attempt to inflict as many casualties
as possible"[1] and that "this is not the same type of bomb that has
been traditionally used by other terrorist groups in the United
States other than the Islamic militant ones."[2] All this was interpreted as my saying point-blank that militant Muslim groups were
involved.

The Council on American-Islamic Relations (CAIR), the American Muslim Council (AMC), and other organizations immediately took offense. Then when Timothy McVeigh was arrested and it turned out domestic terrorists were responsible, Muslim groups claimed they were the real victims. "Surge in hate crimes against Muslims," was the story on the front page of *The New York Times*—based, I believe, entirely on unsubstantiated information fed to them by CAIR. *The Boston Globe, The New York Times,* ABC-TV, National Public Radio—even news outlets that had themselves originally reported that Muslims were among the suspects now took the position that I was the only one who had suggested this. I became persona non grata in many places, including at CBS, which had hired me less than twenty-four hours after the bombing to be a consultant. They ended up blacklisting me for five years. Dan Rather contended, "It was Emerson who misled us."

Still, the news media didn't give up the story themselves. At one point *Newsweek* called up and said, "We'll give you $10,000 to help write our cover story." They were looking for a militant Muslim connection. "Save your money," I told them. "They didn't do it." As soon as the details of the McVeigh arrest emerged, it was obvious that he was responsible and had probably acted nearly alone. Up to that point I had suspected that Islamic radicals were involved. Now I realized I was wrong. I've never wavered from that since then, and I have refused to support the conspiracy theorists who insist that McVeigh himself was actually involved with Muslim groups. But to this day I regret my hasty comments.

Meanwhile, I continued to discover more information at the Investigative Project. People in law enforcement would regularly come to me with new data, records, and documents. The most disturbing were the calls I would get from federal law-enforcement agents who had information and wanted to follow up, but were being prevented by their superiors who weren't interested in these things. More and more, these disgruntled agents turned to us with information that they weren't allowed to pursue themselves.

Our operations became more sophisticated and far-reaching. One of the unexplored mountains of evidence we inherited, for example, was the trial exhibits from the first World Trade Center bombing. Included were the records of thousands of phone calls made by the suspects to the Middle East and other parts of the world. We knew the individuals who were placing the calls, but we couldn't tell who had received them. Yet it was obvious that this was the key to investigating how far the network of international terrorism had extended.

We divided the list of calls up country by country. Then, we engaged a number of Arabic speakers and started making cold calls. Every night at midnight—when the tolls were low and it was daylight on the other side of the world—we would begin dialing numbers in the Middle East. When someone picked up we would engage him in random, nondescript conversation. "How are you? How are things going? I'm calling from the U.S. Do you want to know what's happening here?" One way or another we tried to get them to talk to us.

More than 49 out of 50 calls would be a dead end. The person answering would hang up or wouldn't have any idea of what we were talking about. But that one in fifty proved to be a treasure trove of information. At one point we ended up talking to the son of blind Sheikh Omar Abdel Rahman, the infamous Jersey City imam who plotted a day of terror for Manhattan. Another time we reached the spiritual leader of the Palestinian Islamic Jihad. Little by little it became obvious that all these groups were coordinating their effort in a worldwide network.

Then one day the phone rang, and we hit an absolute gold mine. The caller was a brave Sudanese who was a member of the Republican Brotherhood, a group opposed to Dr. Hassan al-Turabi's fundamentalist regime in Sudan. He was now working as a plumber in Brooklyn. He was in the basement of a building and had just come across scores of boxes of old records that appeared to be the property of Alkhifa Refugee Center, also known as the Office of Services for the Mujahideen, the predecessor to Osama bin Laden's al Qaeda international network. The records had apparently been moved there after the World Trade Center bombing from Alkhifa headquarters at the Al-Farooq Mosque on Atlantic Avenue. He wondered if we would be interested.

We immediately contacted the FBI in New York and Washington. To our utter amazement, they said they couldn't do anything about it. The field agents were very interested but when they ran it up to their superiors, they were told it wouldn't fly. We even smuggled out a few pages to pique their interest but the superiors would not budge. Then we got word that the documents were about to be moved or perhaps even destroyed in about five days.

So we decided to pull off our own covert operation. Our Sudanese contact went into the building at midnight to do his job carrying several large toolboxes. He then immediately emptied the toolboxes and filled them with documents. We met him at the rear of the building in a rented van. We grabbed the toolboxes, each containing about 4,000–5,000 documents, and raced off to a Kinko's in Manhattan where we spent all night feverishly photocopying the material. Then we would race back to the building by 6:00 A.M. and return them to the plumber so he could put them back before the building owners showed up for work. We did this for three straight nights.

The papers contained financial records, address books, information about the fabrication of passports, and countless other materials showing the Alkhifa Refugee Center's involvement in the worldwide jihad movement. When we returned to the building the fourth night, however, our contact didn't show up. We waited and waited but by 7:00 A.M. we were very fearful that something had happened to him. We left and found out later that something had triggered the building owners' suspicion and they had caught him. While we were waiting outside he was being questioned and threatened in the basement. He is a tough guy, however, and somehow got out of it. We ended up keeping the original records instead of copies. Altogether, we only retrieved about one-quarter of the information that was there, but it was great material. We got thousands of leads. Nonetheless, I still think it would have been much better had the FBI gone in.

Although I continue to live at an undisclosed location, I occasionally speak at universities and other public forums. The universities usually provide some form of security but there are never metal detectors. I'm always looking out for somebody who goes quickly into his jacket. One time at Ramapo Community College in New Jersey a group of Muslim protesters rushed the stage. For a brief moment I thought I was finished, but the police restored order. Another time I was speaking at Harvard Law School at a memorial for a twenty-year-old Brandeis University student, Alisa Flatow, who had been killed in Israel in a car bombing carried out by the Palestinian Islamic Jihad. The audience turned out to be 80 percent Muslim. No matter how many times I condemned the Jewish Defense League and Christian terrorists, they continued to bombard me with accusations that I was a racist and anti-Muslim. Up until that point I had thought militancy was a mind-set of impoverished and ill-educated people whose fervor was driven by their lack of opportunity in life. But this was an audience of privileged young people—future doctors and lawyers—and still they openly supported Hamas. This brought home to me that Islamic fundamentalism is a trans-class movement. Poverty and lack of opportunity have little or nothing to do with it. The real proof of militant Islam's trans-class appeal can be seen in the support for the Islamic Fundamentalism among the unions representing doctors, lawyers, and scientists in Islamic countries and in the support for bin Laden in such wealthy countries as Saudi Arabia, Qator, and Kuwait.

Even at my February, 24, 1998, testimony before a Congressional subcommittee on the occasion of the fifth anniversary of the World Trade Center bombing, I had a police escort to and from the hearing room. It was jarring to think that I needed police protection right in the halls of the Senate. Afterward the police escorted me to my car but that was the end of it. They said good-bye and left me on my own.

*   *   *

Less than a year ago, I participated in a seminar at a public agency in Washington where we spent time trying to imagine the worst possible terrorist calamity that could occur in the United States. Two basic scenarios were presented. One individual suggested that the Chinese would launch a nuclear attack using ballistic missiles. Everybody thought that scenario was the most likely. My suggestion was that we would be hit by a much lower-grade attack by Islamic fundamentalists on American soil. Moreover, I said, our response would be constrained because we would not want to offend the sensibilities of Islamic fundamentalist leaders and their groups. They were already establishing a demographic base in both the United States and Europe and would argue strenuously against any kind of effective response.

Unanimously, the other participants responded, "This could never happen." First, they said, fundamentalists would never attack us here. Second, they knew that the U.S. would respond so horrifically if such an event did occur that we would wipe them off the face of the earth. Finally, they said, fundamentalists had no real motive to pull anything like this off.

These were very smart people, dedicated public servants. They had no axes to grind. They weren't arguing the case for one group or another but were sincerely trying to evaluate America's situation as far as international terrorism was concerned. Yet I walked out of that meeting and e-mailed a friend, "We're doomed. It is beyond the official imagination of this government to conceive that we can be attacked. There is a an underlying assumption that we are such good people that nobody would ever want to attack us here." There was nothing venal in their attitude. It just meant our defenses were down. We were turning a blind eye toward the many possibilities for terrorist attack and the militants' infrastructure already in place to help coordinate it. I wanted to grab those people by the lapels and shout, "Don't you see how far this thing has gone already? Don't you realize there are people in this country who hate America and everything it stands for and have absolutely no fear or compunction about doing something about it?"

Since September 11, 2001, everything has changed—and yet nothing has changed. The only difference between February 26, 1993, and September 11, 2001, is that there are 3,500-odd more people dead. We are still vulnerable. We have only a short time to prevent the next chapter from unfolding. This is the most important battle of our time. Today we still have a window of opportunity to prevent further devastation. But the window won't be open for long.

Chapter Two

ANATOMY OF INFILTRATION

O<small>NLY</small> BY KNOWING HOW THE TERRORISTS' NET-
WORKS OPERATE, and what they have accomplished in the past
decade, can we be vigilant in detecting any new activity. Unfortunately, the terrorists' world is complex and shadowy, full of unfa-
miliar names and half-known or hidden activities. In later
chapters I will point out the most important known instances of
American network organization, fund-raising, recruitment, and
operations, but I cannot hope to name every name. Therefore, I
have included in this book several appendices that provide some
basic factual information on the militant fundamentalist Islamist
movement's history and on its support networks here in America.
In the main text, I have focused on discrete pieces of the puzzle, including the three most significant foreign groups on American
soil: Hamas, al Qaeda, and Palestinian Islamic Jihad. I have detailed some of their most successful operations, beginning with

the first World Trade Center bombing in 1993; and the international support they receive from and, in turn, give to countries like Sudan, Egypt, and Afghanistan.

*   *   *

In 1987, FBI informants reported seeing weapons in the Al-Farooq Mosque in Brooklyn. An application for a wiretap was nonetheless turned down by the Justice Department, since there was no evidence of criminal conspiracy. As it turned out, however, the Alkhifa Refugee Center then based at the mosque had become a center for counterfeiting tens of thousands of dollars, shipping explosives to Hamas in the Middle East, reconfiguring passports to enable Muslim volunteers to visit the United Sates, and enlisting new recruits for Jihad in Bosnia, the Philippines, Egypt, Algeria, Kashmir, Palestine, and elsewhere. But at the time, none of this was known.

Two years later, on August 29, 1989, a Connecticut state trooper stopped a suspicious vehicle carrying six "Middle Eastern persons" near the High Rock Shooting Range in Naugatuck. According to FBI reports, the trooper found a small arsenal of semi-automatic weapons and several out-of-state license plates in the trunk. The guns were legally licensed to the driver, a local gun dealer and former Waterbury policeman of Albanian origin. He told police he was training volunteers to fight the Soviets in Afghanistan. A computer check found that the extra license plates were registered to El-Sayeed Nosair, a name that meant little at the time. A year later, on November 5, 1990, Nosair leapt onto the front pages of newspapers when he murdered Rabbi Meir Kahane, the founder of the Jewish Defense League and leader of a militant anti-Arab movement in Israel, at a hotel in New York. By then, several foreign militant movements had moved into the liberal environment of the United States of America. By 1990, Hamas (of Palestine) and al-Gama'at al-Islamiyya (of Egypt) were here, as was the precurser to the now-infamous al Qaeda (of Afghanistan and Sudan) run by Osama bin Laden.

In the following decade, a shifting cast of characters attempted a series of attacks on American targets:

- In January 1993, Pakistani citizen Mir Aimal Kasi shot five CIA employees outside the agency's headquarters, killing two.

- In February 1993, the first World Trade Center bombing killed six and caused over 1,000 others to suffer smoke inhalation. Four men were found guilty, and 118 were listed as potential unindicted coconspirators.

- In June 1993, nine followers of Sheikh Omar Abdel Rahman and the Sheikh himself were arrested in a sting operation, for planning a Day of Terror in New York. They had schemed to bomb the United Nations Headquarters, the Lincoln and Holland Tunnels, the George Washington Bridge, and a federal office building.

- In March 1994, livery driver Rashid Baz opened fire on a bus filled with fifteen Hasidic Jews on the Brooklyn Bridge, killing one and injuring three others.

- In February 1997, a Palestinian schoolteacher opened fire on the observation deck of the Empire State Building, killing one tourist and injuring six others before turning the gun on himself.

- In July 1997, Ghazi Ibrahim abu Mezer was arrested by New York City police, foiling his plan to bomb the subway system.

- On September 11, 2001, nineteen men hijacked four cross-country jetliners, flying two into the twin towers of the World Trade Center which succeeded in collapsing both buildings, and flying one into the Pentagon. The fourth plane crashed in rural Pennsylvania, after passengers foiled the hijackers' plans. Over 3,000 people were killed.

These acts all aimed at Americans at home. But terrorists have also used the country as a base for mayhem committed against other nations and against American targets abroad. Osama bin Laden, for example, used agents in the United States to purchase a satellite telephone and carry it to him, for use in planning the 1998 bombing of U.S. embassies in Kenya and Tanzania. Hamas is known to have sent promising Middle Eastern recruits to the United States for training; here they were taught how to build car bombs and other explosives for use in the Middle East. Above all, the United States has proven a fertile ground for fund-raising. Nonprofit foundations have helped raise untold sums supporting terrorist activities in the Middle East and elsewhere. Overall, the terrorists' activities can be divided into four categories: recruitment, fund-raising and/or money-laundering, networking, and direct organizing.

RECRUITMENT

Foreign terrorist organizations have utilized solo operators in America as well as groups. Some of their representatives and supporters have entered the country illegally, using visa fraud; they have also actively recruited individuals who are able to use American passports to travel freely around the world.

A few examples will give the general idea. For just one example of visa fraud, consider the case of Ghazi Ibrahim abu Mezer. In 1997, he was arrested by New York police acting on a tip, foiling his plan to bomb the city subway system. Abu Mezer had no business being in this country; he had been apprehended on three separate occasions by the Immigration and Naturalization Service within little more than a year prior to his arrest, each time for illegally entering the country from Canada. The INS had begun deportation proceedings, a lengthy process during which abu Mezer was free on bail. He had complicated the matter by applying for political asylum on the grounds that he was in danger of arrest by Israeli law enforcement thanks to his membership in the Hamas organization.[1]

As abu Mezer's example demonstrates, visa fraud is a messy business for terrorists—it is possible, and sometimes even easy, to avoid detention and INS proceedings for months and even years, but if your real name is on a list of suspected terrorists, you must operate clandestinely. Even if the wheels of justice grind slowly, they do grind. Far better, then, for the terrorist organizations is to recruit members who hold American passports. For example, Hamas used Mohammad Salah, an American naturalized citizen, to travel to Israel using his American passport, in order to enter Palestinian territories carrying hundreds of thousands of dollars—primarily from the head of the Hamas Political Bureau in the United States, Musa abu Marzook—to be distributed to Hamas military leaders in the Palestinian territories to help build the military/terrorist infrastructure there. Salah, also known as Abu Ahmed, is a Chicago-based car dealer who was arrested by the Israelis in 1993 while funneling these monies to Hamas terrorists and who was subsequently released in 1997 ultimately to return to Chicago. While he was detained in Israel, he was declared a Specially Designated Terrorist by the Office of Foreign Assets Control of the U.S. Department of the Treasury, and his assets were frozen in 1995.[2] On June 8, 1998, his assets, and those of the Quranic Literacy Institute in Chicago, were seized in a civil forfeiture action by the U.S. Government as proceeds of a Hamas money-laundering operation.[3]

Another example is that of Wadih el-Hage, a forty-year-old naturalized American citizen from Lebanon who worked for al Qaeda and who was convicted in 2001 for the 1998 embassy bombings in Kenya and Tanzania. FBI Special Agent Robert Miranda testified in 2001 at the trial of Wadih el-Hage and others for their roles in the bombings regarding an interview he conducted with el-Hage on August 20, 1998:

> Q: Did he indicate to you why it was that he was asked to work for Usama bin Laden?
>
> MIRANDA: Yes. He said that because he had an American passport, Usama bin Laden wanted him to work for him because he could travel more freely and buy things for bin Laden.[4]

One of Wadih el-Hage's attorneys, Sam Schmidt, emphasized this point even further at the same trial by stating:

> The evidence will show that Wadih el-Hage was hired by
> bin Laden to work in the Sudan, not only because he was
> well-educated, a hard worker, honest, responsible and a
> devout Muslim, but, yes, he was an American free to
> travel throughout the world on an American passport.[5]

Wadih el-Hage served as Osama bin Laden's personal secretary in the early 1990s. In 1994, el-Hage moved to Kenya to set up businesses for bin Laden to be used as terrorist fronts. Mr. Hage's business card shows him as a director of Anhar Trading, a company with addresses in Hamburg, Germany, and Arlington, Texas.

One last example of al Qaeda's use of a U.S. passport holder shows how American residents can use their mobility and access to technology to promote evil. On December 29, 1999, Jordanian authorities arrested "Khalil Ziyad," identified by the FBI as a Florida-based "procurement agent" for Osama bin Laden.[6] His arrest was not publicly revealed by Jordanian authorities and he was later released. But according to U.S. government sources, "Khalil Ziyad" is most likely cooperating with the FBI and providing crucial evidence about the U.S. network of militant muslims. "Ziyad" was to "procure computers, satellite telephones and covert surveillance equipment" for the leadership of bin Laden's organization.[7]

"Khalil Ziyad" is actually known in the United States as Ziyad Khaleel (a.k.a. Ziyad Sadaqa, a.k.a. Ziyad Abdulrahman). Public records reveal that he was associated with a variety of addresses in Orlando, Detroit, Columbia (Missouri), and Denver. Khaleel was also responsible for administering a variety of the most radical Islamic Web sites on the Internet. At various points in the late 1990s, according to Internic/Network Solutions database records, Khaleel was the administrative and billing contact of the official Hamas Web site (*http://www.palestine-info.net*), the Algerian Islamic Salvation Front (FIS) Web site (*http://www.fisalgeria.org*), the Web site of Liberty for the Muslim World (*http://www. lmw.org*), and the *Palestine Times* Web site (*http://www.ptimes. com*). Liberty for the Muslim World, a London-based group, vigorously promotes and defends Hamas, the Muslim Brotherhood, and other terror groups, and republishes much of their propaganda. The *Palestine Times* is a monthly newspaper of the Palestine Information Center, the sponsor of the official Hamas Web site. The official Hamas Web site is regularly updated to maintain a photographic record of Hamas terrorists who have been killed, or martyred, as a result of their terrorist actions. In addition, the Web site contains a section entitled "Hamas Operations—The Glory Record" which details many of the significant terrorist attacks carried out by the Hamas movement since its beginning. Khaleel has given at least one lecture to students at the University of Missouri (Columbia campus) representing the Islamic Association for Palestine (IAP), a group that I discuss at length in Chapter 5.

Until recently, the FBI would not have been allowed to investigate Khaleel. He did not have to tell anyone about his whereabouts. He couldn't be stopped from giving a lecture even if there were suspicions about him. Our freedoms of speech, assembly, and religion are among our most cherished rights, and the Bill of Rights, where these freedoms are enshrined in the First Amendment to the Constitution, is one of the documents that makes America a beacon to the world. What we must understand, however, is that these same freedoms are especially attractive to religious terrorists. We cannot stop anyone from preaching violence short of the "clear and present danger" standard, because we punish deeds, not words. We cannot stop groups from gathering to share their political views, even if one of those views is that the U.S. must be destroyed.

FUND-RAISING/MONEY-LAUNDERING

Much of the terrorists' fund-raising has been the old-fashioned kind: grassroots drives, featuring conferences at which leaders exhort attendees to dig down deep. Representatives of charities dedicated to serving "widows and orphans" of the Middle East conflict make pious appeals; they generally don't admit that they are sending money to the widows of suicide bombers. For example, an organization called the Holy Land Foundation for Relief and Development has been suspected of funneling millions per year to Hamas activists.[8]

Sometimes, according to authorities, the terrorists get more creative. On July 21, 2000, agents from the FBI in Charlotte, North Carolina, charged eighteen people with smuggling contraband cigarettes to Michigan from North Carolina and money-laundering, among other things. What they were really doing, according to authorities, was providing "currency, financial services, training, false documentation and identification, communications equipment, explosives, and other physical assets to Hizballah, in order to facilitate its violent attacks."[9] The media quickly dubbed the group the "Charlotte Hizballah cell." The group's lawyers say that providing aid to Hizballah shouldn't be illegal, since it is primarily a political and religious group. They also say that the case should be limited to a routine cigarette-smuggling claim rather than anything related to counterterrorism statutes.

The suspects were initially accused of fraudulently obtaining visas and of setting up sham marriages. Their main economic activity alledgedly consisted of buying cigarettes in large quantities from outlets in North Carolina and smuggling them to Michigan. Later, authorities charged eight men and one woman with providing assistance to Hizballah. These individuals are accused of planning to purchase night-vision goggles and cameras, stun guns, blasting equipment, binoculars, radars, laser range-finders, mine-detection equipment and advanced aircraft-analysis and design software; they also had wired money between accounts controlled by Hizballah operatives and even arranged life-insurance policies for operatives who might be killed in action. The government, unable to resist the pun, dubbed its sting "Operation Smokescreen." A trial for the nine key players is scheduled for the spring of 2002.

I myself can testify to how widespread grassroots fund-raising efforts are here in the United States. I have been at multiple conferences at which money has been raised for jihad, with passionate speeches that spare few details about the ultimate objectives of the fund-raisers.

NETWORKING

By far the most important tactic utilized by terrorist groups in America has been to use nonprofit organizations to establish a zone of legitimacy within which fund-raising, recruitment, and even outright planning can occur. The use of charitable organizations by jihad warriors and their supporters is a complicated subject. Often, the organizations are perfectly legitimate, but they wittingly or unwittingly provide a forum for evil. Many of these organizations react strongly when accused of collaborating with or facilitating the work of terrorists, for understandable reasons. If their official policy is to oppose and denounce terrorism, how much responsibility must they bear for the contrary behaviors of individual members or guest speakers?

At the meeting of the Muslim Arab Youth Association that I happened upon in 1992, for example, I was at a conference of a group that does very little, at least on the surface. MAYA runs conferences which other groups attend, and where speakers make speeches; it produces and sells an Arabic magazine, *Almujtamaa*, and it helps Muslim youths meet one another. At its Web site, you can download a "marriage application" in English or in Arabic. The organization does not issue many press releases, and those that they do are perfectly respectable. After September 11, 2001, MAYA promptly issued a condemnation of "these apparently senseless acts of terrorism against innocent civilians, which will only be counterproductive to any agenda the perpetrators may have had in mind." The release added the observation that "No political cause could ever be assisted by such immoral acts."[10]

Yet, as I have witnessed firsthand, MAYA's conferences bring together many promoters of hate and violence, and serve as fund-raising opportunities for groups that funnel money to the families of terrorists, perhaps even to the terrorists themselves. I have been accused of anti-Muslim bias for charging MAYA and similar organizations with supporting terrorism. I do not mean to suggest that all members of MAYA are sympathizers, much less collaborators. But I do believe that the organization must take responsibility for what happens at its conferences.

Appendix C of this book will lay out the case against some of the most prominent of such organizations, ones with legitimate-sounding names such as the Council on American-Islamic Relations, the American Muslim Council, or the Muslim Public Affairs Council.

DIRECT ORGANIZING

I should note here, however, that there are also far more purposively sinister organizations in this country. These include a Tampa- and Chicago-based organization run in part by known terrorists of Palestinian Islamic Jihad. Osama bin Laden's al Qaeda network took control of a network of offices dedicated to supporting Afghan mujahideen and refugees, located in over thirty American cities including such major urban centers as New York, Boston, and Tucson.

In some cases, the terror networks have even operated under their own names. One good example is the Advice and Reformation Committee, also known as ARC, set up by a man named Khalid al-Fawwaz. Al-Fawwaz has been indicted by the United

States in association with the bombing of the United States embassies in Kenya and Tanzania in 1998, and the United States is currently seeking his extradition from the United Kingdom in order to put him on trial. Al-Fawwaz was tasked directly by bin Laden to create the Advice and Reformation Committee (ARC) in London to facilitate the propaganda efforts of bin Laden against Saudi Arabia for permitting American troops to be based on its soil. As bin Laden has made clear repeatedly, the American "occupation" of the country in which are located the two holiest sites in Islam, Mecca and Medina, is one of the reasons why he declared jihad against all American citizens. Bin Laden himself is listed on the British articles of incorporation for the ARC.

On December 2, 1998, U.S. prosecutors unsealed documents seeking the extradition of Khalid al-Fawwaz. Among the unsealed documents were two invoices for telephone services billed to the Advice and Reformation Committee that were seized when authorities investigating the bin Laden organization searched al-Fawwaz's London apartment. These invoices bore post office box addresses in Denver, Colorado and Kansas City, Missouri. Despite having at least two United States addresses, the ARC was never incorporated in the United States. If there are other branches of the Advice and Reformation Committee here, they are under no obligation to announce themselves.

Appendix B shows the known organizations that are closely linked to infamous international terrorist organizations. For example, the brother of the head of the Palestinian Islamic Jihad and one of his top deputies (and eventual successor) came to America to help form and run an organization in Tampa and Chicago. On the other hand, the ties between terrorists and many of the groups discussed in Appendix C are far more tenuous. The leaders of the Muslim Arab Youth Association are not suspected to be terrorists—but they are clearly proponents of militant Islam, and their group serves an important function as a venue for radical ideology to be disseminated in the American terrorist infrastructure. To paraphrase Mao, MAYA provides the sea in which the fish swim. But MAYA itself is not likely guilty of any criminal behavior.

I cannot overemphasize that the total number of terrorists in the U.S. is but a fraction of the total number of Islamic extremists, which itself is but a tiny fraction of the total number of American Muslims. There are peaceful and genuinely moderate Muslim-American leaders and organizations here, such as the Islamic Supreme Council of America and the Ibn Khaldun Society. If anything, it is precisely because extremism exists within otherwise legitimate, nonviolent organizations that it must be exposed. The purpose of Appendix C is to show how some of these organizations, even as they pursue "civil rights" and "humanitarian" causes, champion Islamic extremism.

One final bit of perspective: there are over 1,200 mosques in the United States, and anywhere from three to eight million Muslims (the figure is heavily disputed, although new studies clearly indicate the number at the lower end of the range).[11] The vast majority of all American Muslims subscribe to the strong Islamic tradition of tolerance and human dignity. Yet for one key reason, the extremists have disproportionate influence. One prominent cleric argued in 1999 that "because they are active they took over . . . more than 80 per cent of the mosques that have been established in the U.S."[12] Although our pluralist ideals tend to view this statement as an automatic exaggeration, the reality is far more sobering. The vast majority of American mosques are funded with Saudi Arabian money, and most of the funders subscribe to the Saudi doctrine of Wahhabism, an eighteenth-century ideology of extreme purity that supports the spread of Islam through violence. Local imams can be appointed by anyone who chooses to fund and/or found a mosque; hence, the influence of this minority ideology is well entrenched among American clerics.

To see how the potent mix of strident ideology, foreign nationals and American recruits, money, and a modest amount of technological knowhow can produce mayhem, we need look no further than New York City in the early 1990s.

Chapter Three

WORLD TRADE CENTER I

When foreign terror organizations first began colonizing the United States, it was not unreasonable to think that America *wasn't* a target. A great deal of the conferences and publications I monitored in the 1990s concerned fund-raising for Middle Eastern operations. Yet there were clues that Israel wasn't the only western target of Hamas, al Qaeda, et al. Unfortunately, most of these clues were missed.

When El-Sayeed Nosair murdered Rabbi Meir Kahane in New York City, for example, it was thought at first that he was acting alone, a crazed anti-Semite who was trying to take Middle Eastern politics into his own hands. Although the attack was on American soil, Kahane was associated with Israel and Israeli politics, not American institutions. But was he acting alone? And was he really uninterested in America? Hours after he was arrested, police raided his New Jersey apartment and carted away 47 boxes of personal papers. Much of it was in Arabic and appeared to be religious in nature. The contents were ignored—until after the first World Trade Center bombing two-and-a-half years later. Only then did investigators discover what they had missed—a road map of an international terrorist network headquartered in the United States. In a small wirebound notebook, Nosair had written, "We have to thoroughly demoralize the enemies of God by means of destroying and blowing up the towers that constitute the pillars of their civilization such as the tourist attractions they are so proud of and the high buildings they are so proud of." [1] There were cassette tapes of telephone conversations between holy warriors in the United States, Pakistan, and Europe, showing that the American residents were taking orders from abroad. In one conversation, Sheikh Omar Abdul-Rahman, apparently speaking from Peshawar, asked his followers in New Jersey something about an operation involving "camps" in the United States. A man responded, "It was a success. It started Friday evening and ended Monday. It lasted three days and we expect positive results." [2] This was the first indication that terrorist groups were running training camps on American soil. Unfortunately none of this emerged until after February 26, 1993.

At 12:15 P.M. on that day, a huge explosion rocked the bottom floors of One World Trade Center in lower Manhattan. Within seconds smoke was curling up the stairwells of the 110-story building. Thousands of people were trapped on the upper floors. Six people eating lunch in a cafeteria were killed immediately. More than a thousand others suffered injuries ranging from broken bones to smoke inhalation.

The federal investigation of the first World Trade Center

bombing was fast and effective, reassuring Americans that its government could track down domestic terrorists. Furthermore, just a few months after the bombing, another conspiracy to attack multiple targets in New York City was foiled. The popular image of the conspirators in both cases was that they were dangerous but somewhat inept. Only later did it become clear that in both cases there were wide and deep networks of international support behind the assailants.

An initial investigation of the World Trade Center bombing traced the explosion to the B-2 parking level. The blast, an explosion of 1,200 pounds of fertilizer-based urea nitrate compounded with three tanks of compressed hydrogen, had left a gaping hole five stories deep. At the epicenter investigators found fragments of tires, bumpers, pumps, pulleys, frame rails, hinges, and other vehicle parts. Calling in auto experts, they quickly determined that the parts came from a Ford 350 Econoline van. Within days, the investigators found the vehicle identification number on a piece of twisted wreckage. The van was quickly traced to a Ryder truck rental in Jersey City.

The van had been rented the day before the blast by one Mohammed A. Salameh of Jersey City. He had left a $400 deposit. In an apparent attempt at establishing an alibi, Salameh had reported the truck stolen to Jersey City police a few hours later.

One witness at a gas station said that someone answering Salameh's description had filled the tank of a yellow Ryder van there on the morning of the explosion. He had also paid for filling a Lincoln Town Car. Two men of Middle Eastern extraction had been in each vehicle. Police staked out the Ryder agency; astonishingly, two days later Salameh came back to claim his $400 deposit. He was arrested.

FBI agents quickly determined that the owner of the Lincoln was Mahmud Abouhalima, another Jersey City resident who, it would later emerge, had fought in Afghanistan against the Soviets. In the car with him had been Ramzi Ahmed Yousef, who had entered the country six months before, claiming political asylum. Yousef had boarded a plane for Pakistan six hours after the bomb detonated. The fourth man, Eyad Ismoil, had fled to Jordan. Yousef soon emerged as an international link between the assailants and a network of supporters. He had arrived from Pakistan in September 1992 in the company of Ahmad M. Ajaj, a pizza deliveryman in Houston. Ajaj was detained at the airport for carrying three fake passports and other false identification. Incredibly, Yousef was not detained, even though he was by far the more dangerous individual. Yousef had made contact with Salameh within a few days of arrival, and telephone records showed that they called Ajaj frequently over the next six months in New York City, where Ajaj remained in prison. Ajaj seemed to have mysterious connections and unlimited funds. Immediately before deplaning in New York with Yousef he had traveled from Houston to Pakistan to the United Arab Emirates and back to Pakistan.

Also tied to the Jersey City group was Nidal A. Ayyad, a 25-year-old chemical engineer at Allied Signal in Morristown, New Jersey. Ayyad was arrested in his home in Maplewood, New Jersey, on March 10, less than a month after the bombing. Telephone records and interviews showed that he had assiduously approached chemical companies trying to buy the urea-based fertilizers used in making the 1,200-pound bomb. Ayyad had also written a letter to *The New York Times* taking credit for the bombing and demanding that the United States change its policies in the Middle East.

The whole operation had an incredibly amateur flavor. The suspects had not even used false names when renting the truck—a fairly easy process when leaving a cash deposit. The bomb, made from fertilizer and diesel oil, had been constructed by hand in several Jersey City apartments. The ingredients had been mixed in plastic trash barrels. Splashings had left conspicuous stains on floors and ceilings. Yet it was a mistake to dismiss the explosion as amateurish. Among the principal defendants—not to mention the 118 potential unindicted coconspirators named by federal prosecutors—were some highly skilled and highly trained men.

In March 1994, little more than a year after the event, Salameh, Abouhalima, Ayyad, and Ajaj were brought to trial in U.S. District Court in Manhattan. Yousef, still a fugitive, was named a codefendant. The trial lasted five months, involving 207 witnesses and 1,003 exhibits and consuming 10,000 pages of transcript. When Willie Hernandez Moosh, the gas station attendant who filled the two tanks that morning, was asked to indicate the men he had seen, he pointed out two jurors. Nevertheless, the jury had little trouble reaching a verdict. As the forewoman read "Guilty" 38 times, Ayyad shouted "Victory to Islam!" in Arabic and two other defendants began crying out "Allah is great!" One also shouted insults at the jury. Security guards quickly hustled them from the courtroom. The defendants were each sentenced to 240 years in prison.

Yet the verdict left a taste of frustration. Yousef, the apparent professional of the outfit, was still at large. When arrested, Ajaj was carrying a letter of introduction recommending him for training in guerrilla warfare in Pakistan or Afghanistan, suggesting other international connections among the perpetrators. In retrospect it was clear that outside support had come from somewhere. Where had Yousef and Ajaj gotten their money and fake ID papers? How had the defendants found each other in the first place? Writing in *The New York Times,* reporter Richard Bernstein, who had covered the trial, put it like this: "Who wrote Mr. Ajaj's letter of introduction? Why would he have to travel to the Middle East to obtain it? Whom did he see in the United Arab Emirates and Saudi Arabia? Where did Mr. Salameh, who was certainly not a wealthy man, get the $8,400 that he deposited into a bank account he opened jointly with Mr. Ayyad and that prosecutors say was the bankroll for the operation? Did it come from abroad?"[3]

*   *   *

The case dovetailed neatly with another investigation that the FBI had been conducting in the New York area. Concerned about possible terrorist threats, the Bureau had established surveillance over a group assembled around a Jersey City mosque. Presiding was Sheikh Omar Abdel Rahman, a 57-year-old blind Egyptian cleric who had arrived in the United States in 1990 after being acquitted of attempting to assassinate Egyptian president Hosni Mubarak. Sheikh Rahman regularly delivered fiery sermons in which he denounced the United States and Israel and called for a "holy jihad" against America.

Rahman was one of a growing number of Islamic fundamentalists who believe that the secular governments that rule Muslim countries such as Egypt, Saudi Arabia, and Jordan are just as much an affront to true Islam as is the existence of Israel or the influence of the United States over Middle Eastern affairs. Inspired by the Ayatollah Khomeini, these purists have been working to undermine secular governments and assassinate their leaders in Muslim countries around the world.

The FBI planted an informer, Emad Salem, among the Jersey City group. Salem carried hidden microphones and helped the FBI in planting a small video camera, recording the group as it made plans for a Day of Terror. The plan involved simultaneous strikes at United Nations headquarters, the Lincoln and Holland Tunnels, the George Washington Bridge, and the federal office building at 26 Federal Plaza. The recordings were remarkable. In one, four defendants prepared bombs out of diesel oil and fertilizer in a musty garage in Queens. In another, the group rode around Manhattan pointing out various targets and speculating how bombs could be placed to inflict the most damage. In a scene that proved critical, Salem reported to Sheikh Rahman that one of the conspirators had proposed bombing the United Nations, where many Muslim delegates might be killed. "Is this considered licit or illicit?" he asked. "It is not illicit," the sheikh replied, "however it will be bad for Muslims."[4] Then he instructed Salem to find ways to "inflict damage on the American Army itself."[5]

In June 1993, shortly after the World Trade suspects had been apprehended, the FBI swooped in and arrested Sheikh Rahman and nine others, charging them with attempted terrorist acts. One of the defendants turned out to be none other than El-Sayeed Nosair. Even though he had been wounded at the scene at Meir Kahane's murder and treated in the same emergency room, Nosair somehow escaped conviction for murder. He was jailed instead on gun charges. From jail, Nosair continued to plot a campaign of terror. Prison logs show that he met with several of the conspirators in the World Trade Center bombing. "He was a soldier when he shot Kahane and in some ways his status was elevated from soldier to trainer and martyr for the movement,"[6] says Michael Cherkasky, former chief of investigations for the Manhattan District Attorney's Office. "In jail he only became more strident, demanding that the movement go forward. Others took up the mantle."[7] Evidence on Salem's tapes showed that Nosair had been clearly involved in the new plots, and his assassination of Kahane, at first considered the attack of a lone crazed gunman, now emerged as part of a much wider effort. Also appearing regularly on the tapes were Mohammed Salameh, Ramzi Yousef, Ahmad Ajaj, and Nidal Ayyad.

Evidence suggests that Sheikh Rahman had been making plans for a terror bombing even before fleeing Egypt in 1990. In telephone conversations recorded by the militants themselves, he had talked with Nosair and Abouhalima about setting up training camps for Islamic soldiers in the United States. In July 1990, after brief stays in Sudan and Pakistan, Rahman arrived in the United States. His preaching quickly attracted followers at mosques in Jersey City and Brooklyn. Prosecutors argued that these speeches had inspired his followers to begin planning for the assassination of Rabbi Kahane as well as the World Trade Center explosion and other terror bombings. Federal prosecutor Mary Jo White brought charges under an obscure Civil War statute against seditious conspiracy.

Central to the case once again was the elusive Yousef. Sheikh

Rahman had placed several phone calls to an apartment where Yousef lived from 1992 to 1993. In addition, both men had called the same number in Pakistan several times. That number was also found scrawled on a bombing manual that Ajaj was carrying when he entered the country with Yousef.

In the end, the FBI was unable to tie Sheikh Rahman directly to the World Trade Center explosion. They had placed a wiretap on his phone a few weeks before the explosion but nothing incriminating had emerged. Although Rahman advised his followers on specific targets during his speeches, he also attempted to keep his distance, saying he wanted to remain a political leader for Muslims. Defense attorney Lynn Stewart argued strenuously that Sheikh Rahman was being prosecuted for his political beliefs and that his sermons were protected by freedom of speech.

Only four of the nine codefendants in the Day of Terror case testified in their own defense. One said he was training to help Muslims, another that he was preparing to aid Muslims in Afghanistan. A third insisted he knew of no terrorism plans. The fourth, Clement Hampton-El, an American-born Muslim who was wounded while serving as a volunteer medic against the Soviet occupying army in the 1980s, told of his impoverished American childhood. They were all found guilty of conspiracy.

In January 1995, just as the trial was about to begin, Ramzi Yousef was apprehended in Pakistan. Federal agents flew him back to the United States on February 7. During the six-hour flight Yousef bragged of his exploits while disclosing that the World Trade Center bombing had been a seat-of-the-pants operation. He had wanted to use hydroxide, a poison gas, but found it too expensive. The group had rented a Ryder van because buying a truck cost too much money. While feds had suspected that the bombing was timed to coincide with the anniversary of the Persian Gulf war, in fact it had occurred because "the rent was due at the end of the month"[8] and Yousef was anxious to leave the country. After parking the van on Level B-2 and setting the timing device, Yousef, Salameh, and Abouhalima had become trapped behind a truck in Abouhalima's Town Car and feared they wouldn't get out of the garage before the bomb went off.

Eventually they stood on the Jersey City waterfront viewing the carnage. They were disappointed. Yousef had hoped Tower One would fall sideways into Tower Two, knocking over both and killing 250,000 people. When asked his motives, Yousef told Secret Service agent Brian Parr he was retaliating against U.S. aid to Israel. "When I asked why he didn't select Israeli targets, he said they were too difficult to attack. 'If you cannot attack your enemy, you should attack the friend of your enemy.' "[9] The purpose was to let Americans know they were "at war."

Commenting on the verdict, Henry J. DePippo, a former federal prosecutor who helped try the first case, said he doubted the convictions would influence future terrorists. "These are people who are trying to make a statement," he said. "So the punishment, however severe, wouldn't be a deterrent."[10]

*   *   *

The biography of Ramzi Ahmed Yousef that emerged at the trials says a lot about the origins and sophistication of the new terrorists. Yousef is the son of a Pakistani mother and a Palestinian father; he grew up in a working-class Kuwait City suburb. Like many recent terrorists, he is extremely well educated. Yousef speaks Urdu, Arabic, and English, and he studied engineering at Swansea University in Wales from 1986 to 1989. He then went to Afghanistan to be trained in guerrilla fighting at the camps of Osama bin Laden. In 1991 he moved to the Philippines and joined an extreme Muslim group known as Abu Sayyaf. A former deputy commander of the group remembered him as a bitterly anti-American militant who wanted to wage a war of terrorism around the world.

Using a false Iraqi passport, he had come to the United States with a cover story claiming that he was seeking political asylum. He was released pending a hearing. He immediately made contact with the followers of Sheikh Rahman and began seeking recruits in Jersey City. Through the mosque he met Salameh, Ayyad, and Abouhalima and began plotting. Two weeks before the bombing Yousef also called Eyad Ismoil, a Palestinian boyhood friend living in Dallas. Ismoil agreed to come to New York to join the plan. Ismoil was driving the Ryder truck when the group went through the Holland Tunnel on February 26, 1993.

Once he had fled the country Yousef returned to the Philippines, where he became involved in another plot: to kill Pope John Paul II when he visited Manila. He also participated in a plan to blow up eleven American jetliners within 48 hours—a disaster that was only barely avoided by chance. Yousef was experimenting with explosives in his Manila apartment in December 1994 when an accident forced him to flee as smoke billowed everywhere. He left behind a computer with encrypted plans for the hijackings, which experts were able to decode. He was eventually tried and convicted on these charges as well. Although he obviously had enormous financial assistance in buying explosives and circling the globe, Yousef has adamantly refused to tell prosecutors where he got the money.

*　　*　　*

These interconnected plots from the early 1990s tell us at least two things about the new generation of jihadists. First, its aims are broad: the jihadists hate the United States. And as Yousef's membership in a radical Philippine group suggests, they also detest secular or moderate regimes within the Islamic world.

Second, it tells us something about the shifting and elusive nature of terrorists' networks. There are many kinds of networks— from the highly ordered, centralized ones with intelligence at the apex, to highly decentralized ones with the intelligence spread to the periphery. The terror networks are highly decentralized. Any two points can be connected or disconnected fairly easily. Though Osama bin Laden has come to symbolize the source and puppet-master of it all, he is only one among many players. His al Qaeda network has come to serve as something of an umbrella organization, but it would be a mistake to think of it like a corporate holding company. Almost any operator can initiate an act of terror, and find support for it among old and new associates.

Finally, the networks are interconnected in many overlapping ways, which means that a few key nodes can lead experts to many points of potential threat. Consider the connections of one man who bridges the first World Trade Center bombing, *and* the Kahane assassination, *and* the Connecticut shooting ranges, *and* bin Laden himself. This is the story of Ali Mohammed, Osama bin Laden's special-operations man within the United States.

Ali Mohammed was an officer within the United States Army's Special Forces based at Fort Bragg, North Carolina. At the same time, he was arranging for security for meetings between such individuals as Osama bin Laden and Hizballah military chief Imad Mughniyeh in Sudan and coordinating activities with other bin Laden operatives within the United States.

When FBI agents had raided the New Jersey home of El-Sayeed Nosair after his arrest in the shooting of Rabbi Meir Kahane, among the many items found in Nosair's possession were sensitive military documents from Fort Bragg. The documents, some of which were classified Secret, contained the locations of U.S. Special Operations Forces exercises and units in the Middle East, military training schedules, U.S. intelligence estimates of Soviet forces in Afghanistan, a topographical map of Fort Bragg, U.S. Central Command data, and intelligence estimates of Soviet force projection in Afghanistan. Appended throughout the documents were Arabic markings and notations believed to be by Ali Mohammed. Some documents were marked "Top Secret for Training—otherwise unclassified." Other documents were marked "sensitive."

Ali Mohammed was an Egyptian-born Islamic fundamentalist who had come to live in the United States in 1985. He had been in the United States earlier that decade as well, having graduated as a captain from a Special Forces Officers School at Fort Bragg in 1981 in a program for visiting military officials from foreign countries. He joined the U.S. military in 1986 and received a security clearance for level "Secret." He was assigned as a sergeant with the U.S. Army Special Operations at Fort Bragg. He also served unofficially as an assistant instructor at the JFK Special Operations Warfare School; as such he participated in teaching a class on the Middle East and Islamic fundamentalist perceptions of the United States.

Ali Mohammed became active in the war against the Soviets in Afghanistan and soon connected with Islamic militants in New Jersey who had been training and supporting the jihad. Mohammed was introduced to El-Sayeed Nosair by Khalid Ibrahim, an Egyptian-born Islamic fundamentalist in New Jersey. Ibrahim had become active in the Office of Services for the Mujahideen, known as Alkhifa, the group that recruited volunteers and funds for the jihad in Afghanistan. Alkhifa, headquartered in Peshawar, Pakistan, maintained scores of offices worldwide, including three dozen in the United States; its primary American offices were located in Brooklyn, Jersey City, and Tucson, Arizona. According to the U.S. government's indictment against Osama bin Laden and others for their role in the bombing of the United States embassies in Kenya and Tanzania in August 1998, the Office of Services for Alkhifa was transformed into the terrorist organization of Osama bin Laden, known as al Qaeda, around 1989.

According to records of the World Trade Center bombing trials, Ali Mohammed began giving training sessions in New Jersey in guerrilla warfare in 1989 to Islamic militants that included, among others, El-Sayeed Nosair, Mahmud Abouhalima, and Khalid Ibrahim. Other training sessions took place in Connecticut, where Islamic militants trained on weekends. An FBI report, based on Connecticut State Police intelligence, summarized the activities of these training sessions, where semi-automatic weapons were used.

According to military records, Ali Mohammed left the military in November 1989 and moved to Santa Clara, California. Law enforcement officials say he traveled to Afghanistan and Pakistan, where he befriended Osama bin Laden and other top militants in the Islamic fundamentalist movements who had sought sanctuary in Peshawar. From his base in Santa Clara, Mohammed soon emerged as a top aide to Osama bin Laden. Federal officials say that Mohammed traveled regularly to and from Pakistan and Afghanistan, having helped oversee bin Laden's terrorist bases in Khost and other terrorist camps in Afghanistan. In 1991, Mohammed was the person in charge of bin Laden's move from Afghanistan to Sudan. The move was considered perilous since bin Laden had made so many enemies. Mohammed helped bin Laden set up his new home and terrorist base in Khartoum, Sudan, where 2,000 "Arab Afghans"—the name given to the Arab veterans of the Afghanistan jihad—were headquartered in bin Laden terrorist camps. After 1991 Ali Mohammed continued to travel between the terrorist camps in Afghanistan, bin Laden's base in Sudan, and the United States, and continued to train new Islamic recruits in the expanded holy war.

Law enforcement records show that Ali Mohammed's extended stays outside the United States would range from weeks to half a year. But he would always return to the United States, which provided him a safe base from which to travel around the world on behalf of bin Laden. In California, Mohammed became involved in smuggling illegal aliens into the United States, including suspected terrorists. Law enforcement sources say that a favorite route for Mohammed was to smuggle illegal aliens through Vancouver, Canada.

In a seemingly bizarre twist, while in California, Mohammed volunteered to provide information to the FBI on smuggling operations involving other aliens not connected to terrorist groups. Officials say the relationship allowed Mohammed to divert the FBI's attention away from looking at his real role in terrorism into examining the information he gave them about other smuggling. This gave Mohammed a de facto shield, effectively insulating himself from FBI scrutiny for his ties to bin Laden. His relationship with the FBI also helped protect Mohammed from being scrutinized by other federal agencies. Mohammed had also tried to cultivate a relationship with the CIA, which did not succeed, although he had far better success in playing off the FBI against the CIA in his dealings with both agencies. Like a character from a John Le Carré thriller, Mohammed played the role of a triple agent and nearly got away with it.

In late 1994 Ali Mohammed was called by the FBI, who wanted to speak with him about the trial in the World Trade Center conspiracy case. As Mohammed would later state to authorities, "I flew back to the United States, spoke to the FBI, but didn't disclose everything I knew." In other words, Mohammed was continuing to manipulate the American authorities even when he was called to testify regarding the acts of terrorists about whom he possessed information.

Mohammed was named on the long list of potential unindicted coconspirators in the World Trade Center bombing conspiracy released by federal prosecutors. In turn, when Mohammed obtained a copy of this list, he sent it to Wadih el-Hage, bin Laden's personal assistant, in Kenya "expecting that it would be forwarded to bin Laden in Khartoum."

In 1996, according to intelligence reports, Mohammed helped move bin Laden back from Sudan, which wanted to maintain an official arm's-length relationship with Afghanistan (yet keeping its close connections secret). Mohammed continued working for bin Laden in 1997 and 1998, maintaining his role as one of bin Laden's top lieutenants.

In 1998, Mohammed was finally arrested on charges that he was part of al Qaeda, which had been indicted following the embassy bombings in Kenya and Tanzania in that year. On October 20, 2000, Ali Mohammed rendered a guilty plea to all charges filed against him. In his admission, Mohammed admitted his involvement with both the al Qaeda organization and the Egyptian Islamic Jihad organization. He admitted that he had been involved in conducting military and explosives training for al Qaeda in Afghanistan; that he had conducted surveillance of various American, British, French and Israeli targets in Nairobi; that he had trained bin Laden's personal bodyguards to prevent any assassination attempts; and that he arranged security for a meeting between bin Laden and Hizballah military leader Imad Mughniyeh.

*   *   *

As Mohammed's example shows, America is part of an interconnected world of terrorists. The lessons of Mohammed's story are twofold: As noted, a small number of key individuals provide links to many parts of the sprawling network, and the motives of the terrorists are not simply religious fanaticism. Some operatives, like Mohammed, appear to do it for the sake of the intrigue; others do it for the money; some are genuine fanatics; others are unbalanced. The men who shot tourists in the Empire State Building and Hasidic students on the Brooklyn Bridge have been classified as terrorists by the government because they perpetrated violence on civilians for ideological purposes, trying to strike a blow against American society.

In 1993, I only dimly understood these mixed motives. It was not clear to me whether American targets were a top priority of the terrorists. I knew I had to meet them face to face to understand them better. To do so, I had to travel to the fountainhead.

Chapter Four

THE SOURCE

A Journey to Jihad Headquarters

I DON'T THINK THERE'S A WAR HERE, A WAR FRONT HERE IN THE UNITED STATES AT THIS POINT. I THINK IF THE WHOLE SCENARIO CONTINUES THE WAY IT HAS, INEVITABLY THE UNITED STATES IS GOING TO BE REACHING A TYPE OF WAR FRONT. YEAH. BUT NOT RIGHT NOW.

—*Mohammad al-Asi, of the Islamic Education Center in Potomac, Maryland, in a 1994 interview with the author, from the television documentary "Jihad in America"*

WHAT ARE THE ULTIMATE GOALS OF THE TER-RORISTS? What makes them tick? Why do they hate us so powerfully? The international jihad movement is loose and decentralized, but it does flow around the world from certain fertile sources. The sources themselves move—from, for example, Pakistan to Sudan to Afghanistan—yet wherever they are, they inspire and direct hundreds and thousands of followers.

In 1994 I had the chance to meet some of the leaders who at that time were using Pakistan as a base. I was accompanied on this trip by my colleague Khalid Duran.

Before teaching in Germany and America, Khalid spent seven years—1967–1974—teaching Islamic law in Pakistan. He knows the country well. In 1994 Khalid went along with me to meet Hudaifa Azzam, the son of Abdullah Azzam, the legendary Palestinian mullah who was the first to conceive of Islam's international holy war. The visit was arranged through Azzam's nephew, who lives in Chicago. Azzam had begun preaching worldwide jihad from a secure base in Pakistan. As the Afghan war with the Soviets was dying down, he asked, why stop here? The Middle East was full of corrupt secular rulers who had abandoned the true faith. The military training the volunteers from those many countries had received in the hills of Afghanistan would serve as a basis to challenge those regimes. If the U.S.S.R. could be defeated, Azzam argued, so could the U.S.

Someone must have been disturbed by his message. In 1989, Azzam was murdered on his way to Friday mosque services, when his car exploded while winding through Islamabad's narrow streets. Just who murdered Azzam remains a mystery to this day, but his teachings have lived on. His organization was morphed into Osama bin Laden's al Qaeda. But Azzam provided the spiritual cornerstone. I was excited by the prospect of meeting Azzam's eldest surviving son, Hudaifa, only twenty years old when his father was killed.

At the time, the whole Arab world was perturbed by the return of "al-Afghan,"—guerrilla fighters from Afghanistan. They were no longer needed in the Hindu Kush Mountains. Now they were eager to put their practical experience to work in their own countries or anywhere else where they might be able to spread the jihad and their militant view of Islam. Some went to Kashmir, the disputed territory located on the northern frontier between Pakistan and India that is under Indian control, where a guerrilla war had been launched against New Delhi's troops in 1989. In 1993, a few hundred "Afghans" made their way to Bosnia, much to the chagrin of the Bosnian government, which wanted the conflict to be seen as a European issue rather than an Islamic one. But staying in Afghanistan was not an option. In truth, few of the Arab mujahideen had displayed outstanding military skills. Instead they became known for their cruel treatment of prisoners and for tyrannizing the people in the "liberated areas." (These habits have proved their undoing as allied forces have liberated Afghanistan from the Taliban. The Arab Afghans have become isolated and despised by all.)

A number of Arab governments held meetings to discuss this new threat. Algeria, Tunisia, and Egypt felt most intimidated. In the 1920s Egypt had given birth to the Muslim Brotherhood. An offshoot of the Muslim Brotherhood, Al-Jihad, had assassinated President Anwar Sadat in 1981. The civil government was sick of fundamentalists. Algeria had a socialist regime that was equally unacceptable to the zealots. Algerian authorities outlawed the Front Islamique du Salut (Islamic Salvation Front or FIS) in 1992, after it was poised to win Parliamentary elections. Tunisia's progressive democratic government, headed by president General Zinedine ben Ali, felt similarly threatened.

The other black-sheep nation was Pakistan. Many "Afghans" actually spent most of the war in Peshawar, the provincial capital, not far from the border, which became their unofficial headquarters. The local people had soon had enough of these immigrant "Muslim brothers" with their bossy manners—even though Arabs generally enjoy a special respect in this part of the world since they hail from the holy land of Islam and all are considered relatives of the Prophet. The Pakistani Islamist party, Jamaat e-Islami, adopted the Arab Afghans as allies at a time when they had few others. The fundamentalists had never had a very strong popular following, although their doctrine pervaded the Interservices Intelligence Directorate—the "ISI"—which is the real ruler of Pakistan. Now the Jamaat embraced their new "Arab brothers," hoping to capitalize on their prestige.

When Abdullah Azzam was killed in 1989, his two oldest sons died with him. He left behind a large surviving family and a band of dedicated followers, most of whom worked with his "Mektab e-Khidemat Lil-Mujahideen," or "Office of Services for the Mujahideen," a small Arab outpost that published *Al-Jihad,* a monthly Arabic magazine. In the late 1980s and early 1990s that outpost was usurped by Osama bin Laden's al Qaeda organization, which had formed as an offshoot of Azzam's Peshawar-based group.

Handsome in jeans and a leather jacket, Hudaifa looked more like a denizen of Madrid or Naples than a guerrilla warrior. Although as tall as his father, he had nothing of the late sheikh's austerity. The family home was in a suburb of Peshawar, but Hudaifa occupied another house in Islamabad's privileged E-6 sector, where many diplomats and high-ranking Pakistani officials live. This is not to say he lived in grand style. In 1994 the house was divided into two apartments with Hudaifa, his wife, and their newborn son in the rear, living in utter simplicity. The kitchen was a mess, and it was hard to find a clean glass. "We had many guests last night," Hudaifa offered in man-of-the-world style. His wife was nowhere to be seen. The Azzams strictly observed *purdah*, and as males we would never be permitted to see her.

At the time, Hudaifa was a student at Islamabad's International Islamic University, which is housed in the grand National Mosque, a huge tent-like structure with four minarets at the foot of the Margalla Hills, which serve as a backdrop to Pakistan's new capital. Created in the 1960s, Islamabad is still expanding rapidly. The mosque is a tourist attraction, and on holidays large numbers of people assemble there for prayer. On postcards, the building seems grandiose, but in person this impression evaporates quickly. Both the mosque and the university are the accomplishments of General Mohammad Zia ul-Haq, the religious conservative who ruled with an iron fist from 1977 to 1988. The university was the personal brainchild of this man whom the not-so-pious Pakistanis derisively nicknamed their "priest president."

Incorporated into the new university was the Islamic Research Institute, created in 1962 to reform Islamic law and modernize the religion. It quickly became a target of fundamentalist wrath. The "priest president" placed it under the new university's jurisdiction and all thoughts of reforming Islam quietly disappeared. None of this appeared to be known to Hudaifa, who walked past the Institute's front door every day but did not know its history. In fact, most of his classes were taught by Arabs who disguised their sense of inferiority in this environment by staying aloof from Pakistani scholars. Hudaifa, although possessing a fine mind open to fresh impulses, treated the Pakistanis in almost a colonial manner. In the course of our first week, the only materials we saw Hudaifa read were our passports, which he apparently wanted to memorize.

Our visit to the Institute was an emotional reunion for Khalid, who had taught here from 1967 to 1974. Before long almost a dozen of his former colleagues had gathered to welcome him. To our amazement, Hudaifa did not know a single one—nor was he very curious. To him they were all just Pakistanis, with nothing to differentiate a shopkeeper or night watchman from an internationally known scholar. Later he admitted his reservations. He said that most Pakistanis were hypocrites and opportunists. "Nothing remains a secret in this country," he told us. "Everyone takes bribes, without exception." These national and ethnic differences constantly disturbed the utopian concepts of Islamic brotherhood. "The oneness of the *umma* quickly founders once Muslims from one culture are set in another," is how Khalid explained it to me. "The more Islamist they are, the more problems this creates, since the slightest deviation from their own norm is considered a deviation from the pure faith."

The problem that has always faced the jihad is—to use military terminology—an extreme form of "mission creep." The fundamentalists would like the entire world to accept their version of Islam, so no matter where they start, they are always tempted to expand their targets. Hudaifa's contempt for moderate Pakistanis, and his understanding that Muslims from different cultures were at odds, reflected this. Sizing him up, I tried to determine where the bulk of his energies would lie.

Having heard the stories about Arabs indulging in a kind of slave trade, and forcing "unity" on Muslims from different cultures by "marrying" Afghan girls and widows, we gingerly asked Hudaifa about intermarriages. "People are very different," he replied. "With such disparate customs and mentalities, it is not easy to live together. But the jihad has brought Arab brothers from different countries together and made them marry from each other's families." The practice, of course, goes back to the Prophet Muhammad. In fact, a sister of Hudaifa's had been given in marriage to an Algerian, a loyal lieutenant of Azzam and a veteran of the Afghan war and the FIS war on Algeria, now in London. We tried to suggest to Hudaifa that the large-scale population movement among Muslim countries—the influx of hundreds of thousands of Kuwaiti Palestinians into Jordan in the outwash of the Gulf War, for example—would unsettle many of these countries. He did not see the point and was obviously unaccustomed to sociological explanations. In his Manichean vision, the world is divided into good and bad, Islam and the infidels. All Muslims are good, therefore they should get along with each other.

We were ready now to head from Islamabad to Peshawar and the Afghan border. Hudaifa offered to drive us in his black Toyota, his only self-indulgence, and we happily accepted. Hudaifa turned out to be an aggressive driver, but he delivered us safely.

The journey was a historical treat. The Gandhara region was

originally conquered by Alexander the Great, who built the city of Taxila, leaving behind a contingent of soldiers. Maintained for three hundred years, the kingdom was eventually swallowed by the local population, which had adopted Buddhism. It is now the home of some of the oldest Buddha statues in the world—although none as large as the rock statues of Buddha in Afghanistan, which the Taliban destroyed in March 2001. We passed a memorial pillar where our highway crossed the Grand Trunk Road, which once crossed the entire Indian subcontinent. Hudaifa declared that the pillar had been built by Muhammad bin Qasim, the Arab general sent from Baghdad to conquer India in the eighth century. Khalid rolled his eyes and quietly informed me that the pillar was erected by the British in the nineteenth century.

As we passed through Wah, Pakistan's most important center of arms production, Khalid explained that it was a favorite hangout for bandits, who attacked travelers and disappeared into the rugged countryside. I was skeptical. But the next morning the papers reported that robbers had attacked a bus and made off with 200,000 rupees only minutes after we passed through the area.

We arrived at Azzam's family residence in the dark of night. We were greeted at the gate by the night watchman, a ubiquitous figure in Pakistan. From his looks, he was probably a former mujahid. The house didn't look like a fortress or guerrilla headquarters. Inside there was virtually no furniture, just some mattresses spread over a richly embroidered Oriental rug. After being introduced to Hamza, Hudaifa's seventeen-year-old brother, we all squatted on the floor. Hamza, who was attending high school in Peshawar, seemed to think of little else but getting married. Premarital sex is a capital sin in Muslim society, so I suppose I shouldn't have been surprised. He enquired seriously about the daughters of Abu Ayman, his uncle in Chicago who had arranged the visit for us. His questions were so solemn and serious that it was hard not to laugh. We could only tell him that the two daughters we had met were both married. But there was a third daughter, Hamza insisted, who was supposed to be very pretty. (Back in the United States several months later, we actually relayed Hamza's interest to the uncle, who expressed unmistakable approval. Our matchmaking efforts may not have been entirely in vain.)

In Peshawar, even going to the bathroom in a sex-segregated society is difficult. When we informed our host of our needs, he sent word to the women throughout the house to stay out of sight. When I was in the bathroom, I sensed the whole household holding its breath while waiting to return to normal. When I was through, a young man stood waiting to escort me back to the living room.

Hudaifa showed me a photo album of his father. He had quite a few of them. We also saw expressions of grief from the media. Even Pakistan's prime minister Benazir Bhutto had sent condolences—though Azzam had criticized her publicly. After a dinner of delicious Palestinian food, Hudaifa drove us to our hotel.

Next morning Hudaifa took us to the Office of Services, where we met Salih, a Palestinian staff member. He spoke English fairly well and was quite communicative, trying to convert me to his cause. Like Hudaifa, Salih spoke quite favorably of the United States, especially our freedom of religion and expression. Nowhere in the Muslim world, he said, was a believer granted such freedom to live his faith and express his views. The problem, he said, was that the United States supported tyrannical regimes in the Arab world, especially in Israel. Jews, he explained, have too much power in America, controlling our media and shaping national policies.

He also objected to America's immorality, specifically its sexual promiscuity. It's a commonly heard charge; at times it appears to be the Islamists' principal problem. Their main criterion for good and evil in this world is marital fidelity, with virginity as a precondition to marriage. Some of the "Arab Afghans" migrated to Pakistan because they saw their own societies succumbing to sinfulness. On arrival, however, they soon discovered that sinfulness exists here as well, especially in large cities such as Karachi and Lahore. Peshawar was a little more acceptable but still declining. For these pilgrims, Pakistan—which literally means the "Land of the Pure"—was not the Shangri-la they anticipated. In 1996, when the Taliban began to take power in Afghanistan, many of them moved across the border.

Most conversation with jihadists turns sooner or later to children's behavior. In Islam, respect for elders is essential in a way that Westerners can barely imagine. For the Islamist, it is essential in establishing proper relations between the sexes. America can hardly hope to win approval on that score.

That afternoon Salih took us to visit Abu Suhaib, a young editor of *Al-Jihad,* Azzam's monthly magazine. Suhaib was somewhat suspicious of our unanticipated arrival. He told us he had no desire to visit the United States and criticized American life as excessive in its libertinism and negative effects on children. We explained that the Catholic school Khalid's eldest daughter attended in Chicago was hardly different from the ideal Muslim school. Suhaib registered this information without interest. He had visitors outside but dismissed them, obviously interested in us despite his aloofness.

We were impressed with the production facilities of *Al-Jihad* and wondered how Suhaib did it all himself. He put us off with sincere modesty. "But what about the future?" we asked. "Aren't you threatened with expulsion, given all the pressure the various Arab capitals are exerting on the Pakistani government?"

"There is nothing to be afraid of," responded Suhaib. "If we are expelled, we will return to Jordan. Each of us has his profession. Most of us had good jobs before. We are members of the educated class."

"But won't you miss the life of a mujahid?" pursued Khalid. "Here you have a mission and a sense of purpose. Won't it be boring to go back to your old life?"

Abu Suhaib, visibly moved, admitted all this to be true. Behind his equanimity he obviously hoped the war would continue somewhere.

The Arab Afghans we met in Peshawar seemed a milder brand. The tougher ones had all left for Sudan and Yemen, with the most active breed fighting in Kashmir, Bosnia, and Somalia. In addition, fierce fighting was now raging between rival factions in Afghanistan. A few adventurers had moved on to Tajikistan, which promised to be a new Central Asian battleground.

Those who stayed behind were potential settlers. They already had their own infrastructure, with school and community centers. Hamza, Hudaifa's younger brother, for example, did not attend a Pakistani school. His high school was all Arabic, a product of the Afghan war. The mosque where Azzam had preached his sermons before being blown up had also become a school for the Arab community. Before the war there were no Arab schools in Peshawar.

Tapes show how the elder Azzam would captivate an audience, weaving his account with mesmerizing detail. Hudaifa does the same thing. Like his father, Hudaifa is a storyteller in the tradition of *Arabian Nights.* He told us the story of a Libyan mujahid who became one of the first Arab martyrs to die in Tajikistan, mowing down rows of his enemies even after he had been mortally wounded. Hudaifa's English seemed to be getting better and better with each episode. He obviously enjoyed talking with us, even though he did not fully trust us. Overall, I thought he seemed far more attracted to the United States than to Pakistan.

Hudaifa confided his problems with his Jordanian passport. It was about to expire and the Jordanian embassy seemed unwilling to renew it. They wanted him to return home. He did not fear jail, even though he would certainly end up there—moderate Islamic governments being much less tolerant of fundamentalism than we are. But he still wanted to travel abroad. We asked him if he would like to come to the United States, where so much of his family has settled. He seemed to like the idea but felt obligated to continue his father's work. Strangely, he was much more interested in talking with me than with Khalid. While he had been around Muslim scholars like Khalid all his life, I was a curious American journalist runaway from the Great Satan.

The next day Hudaifa showed us the entire jihad organization, including a fairly large compound with ten printing presses. The laborers were all Afghans, the headmen Palestinians. There were no educated Afghanis or Pakistanis around. More and more I realized that he was living in a vacuum with only a few devoted natives, without the rallying support that his father enjoyed before his death.

Hudaifa was not the boss of the show, however. The headman was Muhammad Yusuf Abbas, commonly known as Abu l-Qasim, who was suspicious and angry to find us in his office. He gave a scolding to Hudaifa, who remained remarkably calm, holding his ground without perplexity or embarrassment. Abbas was finally reassured of our purpose and, in the end, he even agreed to be tape-recorded.

"Why has jihad become necessary?" I asked him. "Is it an obligation to Muslims everywhere?"

"After Afghanistan it has spread to many places," he replied. "It has spread to Kashmir, the Philippines, Algeria, and Bosnia and has grown stronger in Somalia since the U.N. intervention."

Why is jihad necessary in Muslim countries like Egypt and Algeria? Does it make sense for Muslims to be killing Muslims?

"In the countries that used to follow Islam, the so-called Muslim countries, the jihad movement has arisen because they have been deprived of Islam. Western colonialism ruled those countries without Islam and the liberation movements were unable to restore Islam to its rightful place. Muslims have finally become aware of this point. Now everywhere they want Islam."

What are the teachings of jihad? Should it go west? Is it the role of Muslims to carry out jihad everywhere?

"The Islamic teaching about jihad says that it is to clear the way for those calling to God's religion. Wherever the missionaries of Islam are fought against, it becomes necessary for the Muslim power to protect them."

In so many words, the answer was that America and the West were new arrivals on the target list, as legitimate a target as Israel or the secular regimes of the Muslim world. Jihad would follow wherever the warriors went.

*   *   *

The next day, Hudaifa suggested we take a trip to the Khyber Pass. Once again we piled into the Toyota. As it turned out, Hudaifa meant a trip to the Peshawar exit to the Khyber Gate, which is on the border of the tribal areas, only loosely associated with Pakistan. Foreigners needed a special permit to enter there.

At the checkpoint, Hudaifa, at our behest, tried to rush through over the protests of the militia guards. Using all his broken Pashtu, he played strongman, trying to impress them with his invisible authority. The guards were polite and apologetic but firm. They were only doing their duty and might get in trouble with their superiors. Finally, realizing there was no point in having a confrontation, Khalid pulled their officer aside and explained in Urdu—the government language—that we just wanted to go a few hundred yards to take some photos. He immediately agreed.

One of the militia accompanied us. Upon learning Hudaifa is

Palestinian, he immediately said, "PLO," to which Hudaifa replied, "No, Hamas!" Surprisingly, the militiaman didn't seem to recognize Hamas.

Unable to go as far as Dara, the region's famous arms bazaar, or Landi Kotal, a smugglers' paradise where Pakistanis go to buy electrical appliances and other goods, we settled for a small outdoor market near the Khyber Gate. Here it was all in miniature— small shops filled with smuggled clothing and TV sets plus weapons from all of the world, some duplicated by Afghan tribesmen in primitive workshops. Seeing a local manufactured Kalashnikov knock-off, Hudaifa could hardly contain himself. He rented it for a half-hour for the pleasure of firing a few rounds in the air. "I haven't done that in more than a year," he exulted. I took photos of this trigger-happy international revolutionary. Then Khalid almost burned himself handling the gun. Hudaifa explained that that was the difference between the local varieties and the real thing; the Russian guns generated much less heat.

We returned to Peshawar just in time for Friday prayer services at the mosque. The sermon was over but we did catch the prayer. The majority of the faithful at this overcrowded mosque were Pakistani but there were about forty Arabs among them. Most were members of Azzam's organization. As we left the mosque, two Sudanese passed us, then turned back and shook hands, greeting us in Arabic with special friendliness.

Hudaifa, now accompanied by his brother Hamza, pulled us into a group of his followers and suggested we visit his uncle, Abu Adil, another important survivor of Azzam's group. We would have lunch at his house before catching our plane back to Islamabad at five o'clock. When we arrived at the house, however, Hudaifa informed us that his uncle was renting it from Gulbuddin Hekmatyar, the Afghani fundamentalist then serving as the new prime minister of Afghanistan. Khalid had denounced Hekmatyar many times in the international Islamic press. Several of his friends in Peshawar had actually been killed in retribution by Hekmatyar's commandos. He was now horrified to realize we would be having lunch in Hekmatyar's house. "It's not that I'm afraid," he confided to me. "But it would be terribly unethical." But Khalid was trembling.

As it turned out the food was not ready so we had an excuse for not staying long. The suburban villa was actually an oasis of ease compared with the mud huts that constituted most refugee settlements in and around Peshawar. Squatting on the floor, we asked Abu Adil how he felt about the open warfare that had erupted between Hekmatyar and President Rabbani, who had emerged as his chief rival. (Both sides were using the tanks and artillery left behind by the CIA and KGB to hammer each other.) Abu Adil responded by showing us photographs in which Hekmatyar, Rabbani, and Azzam stood with their arms locked in Islamic brotherhood. "We knew them only as mujahideen," he said. "Now they are statesmen."

Hudaifa, Abu Adil, and the immediate family were all jovial and lighthearted, in contrast to some of the other fundamentalists we met earlier that day at another mujahid home in Peshawar. They were dour and tense, exuding unrelenting distrust and hostility. They even slept with their Kalashnikovs. We sensed how rudderless the group had become without Azzam. Whenever we brought up the name of another potential leader with Hudaifa, he immediately dismissed him. The others always agreed. Only two names struck a positive chord: Osama bin Laden and Wa'il Jalaidan. Bin Laden was in Khartoum at the time. Jalaidan, another Saudi, was nearby in Islamabad. He had been put in charge of the Pakistan office of the Muslim World League, a worldwide Islamist organization richly funded by the Saudis. When we expressed interest in Jalaidan, Hudaifa promised a meeting the next day, before our plane left for Syria. But in the end he was unable to arrange it.

Jalaidan has since been described by U.S. authorities as "one of the founders of al Qaeda along with Osama bin Laden" and as "the logistics chief of Bin Laden's organization." He remains essential to the organization.[1] When the American-led coalition attacked al Qaeda in 2001, graffiti in Pakistan on Islamic schools proclaimed, "Kill one Osama, 100 other Osamas will take his place." Jalaidan would be a possible candidate. Ironically, prior to his indoctrination into the jihad leadership in Pakistan and Afghanistan, Jalaidan lived and worked at the Islamic Center of Tucson. Eight years ago in Islamabad, we barely missed meeting him.

*　　*　　*

Saturday morning just before we flew out, Khalid visited the Bosnian embassy to call on the parents of Bosnian prime minister Haris Silajdzic, with whom he had lived in Sarajevo in the 1950s. It was an emotional reunion. The old man, Hafiz Kamil Silajdzic, was once the imam of Bosnia's biggest mosque. The elder Silajdzic represented Islam at its best. This venerable tradition has no more relevance to Islamic fundamentalism than the ranting of Hitler had to the traditions of Western civilization. Both are totalitarian corruptions of a proud heritage. To the militant fundamentalists, Islam's long history of learning and community is as alien and as irrelevant as American TV.

Chapter Five

HAMAS

The Original Infiltrator

To UNDERSTAND HOW the jihad movement has made full use of American hospitality, it helps to examine a single chain of organizations with as much unity of purpose and operations as possible. Searching for a source of terror in America, many people have pointed fingers at al Qaeda, whose first outposts here were set up in the late 1980s. Yet there is another organization, familiar from countless headlines stemming from terrorism in the Middle East, that has flown under the media's radar in the wake of September 11, 2001: Hamas. Hamas's aims may seem more modest; no international Hamas celebrity has reached the status of Osama bin Laden, let alone declared that all U.S. citizens are legitimate targets. Yet Hamas is extremely well entrenched in the United States, and the interlocking operations with which it is associated are extraordinary in their reach.

Hamas is world famous as the main Islamist organization in the Palestinian territories. Yet it is a relatively recent organization, formed immediately after the *intifada* of 1987. Hamas not only opposes the Middle East peace process, it seek's Israel's destruction. It has a political and a military wing; the former builds schools and hospitals in Palestinian territories. Graduates from its political wing earn the right to carry out terrorist attacks against Israeli targets.

Of all the Islamic militant groups, Hamas has developed the most sophisticated American infrastructure. The story of how a young man named Nasser Issa Jalal Hidmi was recruited and trained by Hamas illustrates just how central is the American role in Hamas's network. I have been able to reconstruct Hidmi's story by studying documents retrieved by Israeli investigators and confessions to Israeli courts by various Hamas operatives and the recordings of Hamas conferences in the U.S.

As a student in a Jerusalem preparatory college, Hidmi joined an Islamic religious group that served as a nursery for future military operatives. Motivated by a strong antipathy to the Israeli occupation, he was introduced to a cleric who went by the *nom de guerre* of Abu 'Ubaada and who supervised a wing of Hamas terror squads. In a short time, Hidmi showed promise as a rising Hamas star. The organization's leaders needed a safe place to send him for training. Rather than Lebanon or Syria, he was sent to the United States.

In June 1990, only months after arriving in the United States and settling in Manhattan, Kansas, Hidmi received a phone call from Mohammed Salah, the Chicago-based used-car dealer who was subsequently imprisoned by the Israelis. Per Salah's instruction, Hidmi flew to Chicago where he was one of twenty-five other Palestinian youths selected for a week-end of terrorist training at a campground on the outskirts of the city.

In their Hamas "basic training" course, the recruits were given instruction in Islamic religious issues—but also in the planting of car bombs. The car-bomb instructor identified him-self as a Libyan-American man who had previously served in the Marines and was married to an American woman. Using charts and diagrams, the instructor showed how to place a bomb in a car's engine and how to insure its detonation at the point of ignition. The first stage of the training completed, the students returned home.

Later that year, Hidmi and the other Hamas inductees were told to attend an Islamic convention in Kansas City. For these young militants, the presence of so many Hamas leaders in one place—let alone the United States—was startling. During the next three days, numerous top officials exulted in the opera-tions of Hamas, reveling in the glory of the burgeoning international Islamic movement and railing against the crusader-Zionist-infidel conspiracy being carried out by the perfidious Jews.

Though the gathering was in America, and many of the speakers lived in this country, their targets were international. Musa abu Marzook, a resident of Falls Church, Virginia (and sep-arately, Louisiana), was one major Hamas leader who spoke there.

He called upon Muslims to destroy the "outpost of Western influence" that was created with the "purpose of being a spearhead in the heart of the Muslim world"—i.e., Israel.

During the conference, Mohammed Salah organized a series of smaller workshops for Hidmi and other Hamas recruits at a nearby Ramada Inn. At the front of a room, a burly man introduced himself as Ibrahim Mahmoud Muzayyin, director of an organization called the Holy Land Foundation for Relief and Development, which officially raises money for "charity" in the West Bank and Gaza. Muzayyin told the group: "You have been assembled here because you are all residents of the occupied territories. And you have been chosen to carry out operations to escalate the *intifada* on behalf of the Hamas movement." [1]

One noted Islamic militant at this session was Jordanian parliamentarian Ishaq al-Farhan, who gave the students a pep talk. Al-Farhan had been found by Jordanian security forces to have collaborated with a Hamas leader in Jordan in acquiring weapons for the group in Gaza. Another was Najib al-Ghosh, editor-in-chief of the Muslim Arab Youth Association's flagship magazine, *Al-Amal*, published out of Plainfield, Indiana.

After a series of pep talks, the group was divided into smaller clusters for their car-bomb lessons. They also learned how to handle improvised explosives and hand grenades. In other parts of the conference, the youths were segmented into areas of specialized training, including interrogation and execution of collaborators, surveillance, and political organizing.

Six months later, the group met again in Kansas City. Mohammed Salah introduced Najib al-Ghosh, who lectured on the methods of interrogation of Israeli intelligence as well as on the different types of hand grenades and bombs. "The purpose of all this," Salah interjected, "is so that everyone will go home and plant explosives in the area where he lives." [2]

Before Hidmi had a chance to plant explosives, he was arrested on his return to Israel. More than a dozen of the original twenty-five from Hidmi's class still remain in the United States. In early 1993, chief organizer Salah was arrested by Israeli authorities on a visit to Israel while arranging Hamas terror operations. When news of his arrest was first reported, including the fact that he was a military commander of Hamas, the FBI (as well as American media) dismissed the allegations skeptically. "We were wrong," says former FBI Director of Counterterrorism Oliver "Buck" Revell. "We didn't know what was going on in our own backyard." During his interrogation—conducted in Arabic—Salah confessed to making several surreptitious trips to Israel, where he directed Hamas terror operations, organized military cells, and transferred more than $1 million for the purchase of weapons. Other information obtained by Israeli authorities confirmed that since 1987, Salah had recruited hundreds of Hamas operatives, trained them, and personally built fourteen time bombs. Salah kept a map showing where two kidnapped Israeli soldiers had been buried by Hamas death squads.

Hamas's success in planting some of its most senior military officials in the United States provides some of the most compelling evidence of the deep roots of radical Islamic networks on American soil. One of those officials, Musa abu Marzook, provided Salah's instructions for his incursions into Israel to provide funds to Hamas operatives within the West Bank and the Gaza Strip. Abu Marzook has been one of the highest-ranking officials in Hamas ever since its inception, and used the United States freely as a base to organize and plot terror operations on and off for fifteen years. Today he lives in Syria and appears frequently as a spokesman for Hamas's political bureau. But his formative years as a terrorist and organizer were spent here.

Abu Marzook was born in 1951 in the town of Rafiah in the Gaza Strip. He earned a college degree in engineering in Cairo in 1975 and soon moved to Louisiana to get his doctorate. By the early 1980s, abu Marzook had become increasingly involved with a growing community of militant Muslims in the United States, whose worldwide ideological fundamentalist fervor was unleashed by the Iranian revolution, the assassination of Anwar Sadat, and the jihad against the Soviet occupation of Afghanistan. Together with several colleagues, abu Marzook helped create an umbrella organization called the Islamic Association for Palestine (IAP); abu Marzook would be elected head of the group's "Majlis al-Shura" or consultative council, which oversaw all of the group's activities. By the mid-1980s, several years before Hamas came into formal existence in December 1987, the IAP had established offices in Indiana, Arizona, Illinois, and California and published a militant magazine called *Ila Filistin* (which routinely called for the death of "infidels and Jews"). Internal Hamas documents strongly suggest that the 1988 Hamas charter—a virulent anti-Semitic conspiratorial tract that incorporates elements of both Nazi dogma and the notorious turn-of-the-century "Protocols of the Elders of Zion"—was first written by members of the lAP in the United States in the early to mid-1980s.

In 1989, abu Marzook became the founding president of the United Association for Studies and Research (UASR), which incorporated in Illinois. Four years later, one detainee would tell Israeli authorities that UASR acted as "the political command of Hamas in the United States."[3] The executive director of UASR, Ahmed bin Yousef, who consistently denies any leadership role in Hamas, was also named by this detainee as a "Hamas leader in the United States." Not surprisingly, bin Yousef, prior to joining UASR, was employed by the Islamic Association for Palestine as a journalist with both their English and Arabic-language publications.[4] Bin Yousef has also edited a popular book about Hamas's founder and leader entitled *Ahmed Yassin: The Phenomenon, the Miracle, and the Legend of the Challenge.*[5] It contains odes of praise and letters extolling the imminent victory of Hamas over the Jews. One letter to the Hamas fighters in Palestine is from a Hamas activist in Chicago: "Greetings to you from here in America, from over the seas, that you may know that we are your sons of the era, the era of Allah, the era of Islam, the era of Palestine, the era of Jihad, the era of Hamas, until complete liberation of all Palestine from the river to the sea!"[6]

In a UASR pamphlet by Ahmed bin Yousef called *Hamas: Background of Its Inception and Horizons of Its March,*[7] Hamas is glorified as being the only solution to the conflict between the Palestinians and the Israelis: "Verily Hamas is the only way of dealing with the nature of the conflict, distinguishing itself from the other forms of confrontation, given the fact that Allah has promised that in the Muslims fighting the Jew, the Muslim would be victorious."[8]

In June of 1991, in Herndon, Virginia, the UASR joined with

the Virginia-based International Institute for Islamic Thought (IIIT) to cosponsor a conference entitled "The Islamic Movement in the Shadow of International Change and Crisis in the Gulf." UASR published a monograph of the proceedings of this conference which reads like a *Who's Who* of radical Islamist leaders worldwide. Presenters included Musa abu Marzook, Ramadan Abdullah Shallah and Sami al-Arian associated with the Palestinian Islamic Jihad (see Chapter 6), Ishaq al-Farhan of the Jordanian Islamic Action Front (who had also attended Nasser Hidmi's training sessions), and, of course, UASR's own Ahmed bin Yousef.

The connections between Musa abu Marzook and the UASR (and Mohammed Salah) were further underscored when court documents surfaced in Chicago in June 1998 pursuant to a civil forfeiture of $1.4 million in bank accounts and other assets belonging to Salah and a related charitable organization, the Quranic Literacy Institute. An affidavit filed by FBI Special Agent Robert Wright alleged that Nasser al-Khatib—who was described as abu Marzook's "personal secretary"—had transferred the funds to Salah that Salah had distributed to Hamas activists in the Middle East.[9] Al-Khatib left the United States in June 1993, but upon his return he was interviewed by the FBI. In that interview al-Khatib admitted that he was a supporter of Hamas, that he donated money to Hamas causes, and that he was returning to the United States in order to begin work with UASR.[10]

While continuing to use the United States as his base, abu Marzook eventually took on the title of Head of the Political Bureau of Hamas. In this position, he traveled to and from the Middle East frequently. All that changed, however, on July 25, 1995, when he was detained at JFK International Airport. A routine inspection by an INS agent revealed that abu Marzook's name and date of birth matched a database entry on a "terrorist watch" list. He was under indictment in Israel for conspiring with other Hamas members in a series of at least ten incidents, in which at least 47 people died and 148 others were injured. Among the incidents were two bus bombings and some stabbings. Israeli documents stated that he not only knew about such activities but was integrally involved in providing the funds for them; it was he who gave the go-ahead for the murders. Part of the Israelis' evidence came from Mohammed Salah, who by this point had given evidence against Marzook.

On August 7, 1995, the Deputy U.S. Attorney for the Southern District of New York requested abu Marzook's arrest and extradition. Extradition hearings proceeded slowly until April 1997, when Israel announced it would no longer seek abu Marzook's extradition (no doubt out of fear of a backlash). Nonetheless, with proof of abu Marzook's connections to actual terrorist acts, the United States deported him to Jordan. In 1999, Jordan's King Abdullah II announced that the Hamas leadership in Jordan, including abu Marzook, would in turn be deported. After moving from country to country in the Middle East, abu Marzook finally settled in Syria.

At the time of his airport arrest, abu Marzook was carrying an address book that "contain[ed] the names, telephone numbers, and addresses of several known active and violent terrorists and terrorist organizations," according to FBI Special Agent Joseph Hummell.[11] More than 20 percent of abu Marzook's addresses

were American. Abu Marzook was also carrying paperwork showing his business companies to be worth more than $10 million,
which law enforcement officials suspected to have been part of a
Hamas American money-laundering operation. In response to his
arrest, a Gaza Strip group calling itself "Students of Musa abu
Marzook" distributed leaflets in September, 1995, with an omi-
nous "warning for every dirty American who lives in our beautiful
country." [12]

The organizations founded by abu Marzook are those most
closely associated with Hamas in the United States. These include
IAP and the UASR. In the late 1990s they were joined by the Holy
Land Foundation for Relief and Development (HLF), originally
founded as the Occupied Land Fund and heavily funded by Marzook. [13] According to its English-language brochures, HLF solicits
tax-deductible donations for charitable causes such as "needy
Palestinian children, health clinics and schools." Although much
of the money is spent accordingly, substantial funds are routed
though Hamas's municipal *zakat* (fund-raising) organizations in
the West Bank and Gaza. These zakats function as incubators and
purveyors of radical Islamic ideology, indoctrinating Muslim
youths as well as covertly providing money to Hamas military
squads.

The IAP claims it does no fund-raising for activities outside
the United States. However, internal materials, videos and documents show that it operates an extensive network carefully designed to reach different audiences, from Hamas believers to
secular Americans. With offices and affiliates in more than a dozen
cities, IAP is a public-relations machine. In addition to publishing

newspapers, it has produced terrorist training and recruitment videos that show actual terrorists boasting of their "kills" plus grisly interrogations of "collaborators" just before their executions. IAP also disseminates "moderate" videos for American audiences. It has sponsored a traveling Hamas musical troupe that has penned, among many original lyrics, a song with the refrain, "We buy Paradise with the blood of the Jews." IAP also has operated jihad summer retreats for adults and children.

Fund-raising, on the other hand, has been relegated to the Holy Land Foundation.

Ronni Shaked, a former official in the Israeli General Security Service, commented on Hamas fund-raising in a book he wrote (published in 1994 in Hebrew) based on his interviews with operatives while they were imprisoned:

> The major channel for fund-raising for the Hamas organization in the United States is the Occupied Land Fund that was established in Los Angeles, California. In 1992, the organization changed its name to the Holy Land Foundation and moved to Richardson, Texas.[14]

In December 2001, the assets of HLF in America were frozen by presidential order. According to a memo dated November 5 by FBI Assistant Director Dale L. Watson, the FBI had been gathering evidence of HLF's ties to Hamas since 1993, and "a majority of the funds collected by the HLFRD are used to support HAMAS activities in the Middle East." It was all carefully planned. At a meeting in October 1993 at a Marriott hotel in Philadelphia that the FBI secretly recorded, five Hamas leaders met with the top three executives of HLF: Shukri Abu Baker, the chief executive, Haitham Maghawri, the executive director, and Ghassan Elashi, the chairman. As Watson summarized, "It was decided that most or almost all of the funds collected in the future should be directed to enhance the Islamic Resistance Movement and to weaken the self-rule government," i.e., what later became the Palestinian Authority. "Holy War efforts should be supported by increasing spending on the injured, the prisoners and their families." According to the FBI, the participants agreed that "In the United States, they could raise funds, propagate their political goals, affect public opinion, and influence decision-making of the U.S. government." [15] One reliable FBI source reported that at a 1994 IAP conference in California, the HLF's CEO, Shukri Abu Baker, was introduced to the audience as a senior vice president of Hamas. [16]

At a 1994 meeting in Oxford, Mississippi, recorded by the FBI, the role of HLF was affirmed when Hamas members met with a competitor, Abdelhaleem Hasan Ashqar, head of the al-Aqsa Educational Fund, to explain that "Mousa Abu Marzook designated the HLFRD as the primary fund-raising entity [for Hamas]." [17]

The offices of the HLF in Israel were closed by the Israeli authorities in May 1997 and again in December 1997, based on the connection between HLF fund-raising and support for Hamas. When the office in Jerusalem was closed, an orphan support form was seized for a child named Bar'a Ayyash. This child's father, Yahya Ayyash, was best known for his exploits on behalf of the Hamas movement as its primary bombmaker and strategist. Nicknamed "the Engineer," Ayyash was killed in early 1996 when his cellular telephone was booby-trapped with a bomb.

His funeral was attended by thousands, and the support provided by HLF to Ayyash's family is indicative of the type of support that HLF provides to Hamas. By giving money to the family after the Hamas terrorist's demise, HLF encourages others to engage in similar terrorist conduct by ensuring that the terrorists need not fear for the well-being of their families after they have died for their cause.

HLF's Jerusalem office chairman, Muhammad Anati, was arrested and indicted on charges of aiding and abetting a terrorist organization. Exactly whom HLF supported was addressed in statements made to Israeli authorities by Anati. As he explained:

> I remember I used to send to the United States—pictures of orphans, photos of projects that we did, photos of refugee camps and also videos that used to arrive to videotape projects, refugee camps, and photos of historical places, such as the Machpelah Caves in Hebron, Jerusalem, etc. . . . They used to present the movies and the photos in front of the people in the United States— invited them to conferences to show these movies. During these conferences, they used to describe the organization—The Holy Land Foundation, about the charity, they used to describe it as an Islamic organization which helps people. They did not say directly that the organization supported Hamas, they told the people that the institute—The Holy Land Foundation—is an Islamic institute, which was connected and was supporting Hamas.[18]

Donations to the HLF were transferred not just to HLF Jerusalem (prior to its closure) but to a variety of organizations in the occupied territories and Palestinian Authority–controlled areas either affiliated with or sympathetic to Hamas.[19] For example, the Israelis found a master list of payments made by the "Muslim Youth Society" in Hebron, one of the HLF's charities. The list is divided into six columns: the name of the "martyr" (a Hamas operative who was killed), the "martyr's" chief benefactor, the benefactor's identity number, his/her relationship to the "martyr," the amount paid, and the signature of a Muslim Youth Society official. The list is extensive, illustrating the reach of HLF funds. By using the Muslim Youth Society as an intermediary, the funds did not appear to go directly from the HLF to Hamas operatives, or Hamas-affiliated persons.

Among the "martyrs" on the list:

- Eiyad Hasin Abdal Aziz Hadid: Involved in the murder of the Lapid family on December 6, 1993. He was killed by the Israeli Defense Forces on March 24, 1994.

- Marwan Muhammad Halil abu Ramila: Involved in the attack on Ephraim Zrviv in November 1993. He was killed by the Israeli Defense Forces on March 24, 1994.

- Khatem Kader Ya'akov Makhtaseb: An activist with the Izz al-Din al-Qassem brigades of Hamas (the units responsible for the suicide bombings carried out by Hamas) who was involved in a shooting against the Israeli Defense Forces.

Similarly, when the FBI analyzed documents seized by the Israeli government during a May 7, 1995, search of the HLF office in the village of Beit Haucha, the Bureau found lists of over fifty recipients of the HLF and with Hamas corrections parents, wives, and siblings of terrorists. FBI assistant Watson notes that "It is the FBI's analysis that the documents seized demonstrate the control the HLFRD Headquarters in Richardson, Texas, had over the HLFRD Jerusalem office."

*　　*　　*

The Israeli court documents describe how the HLF prioritized its funding. The Israeli General Security Services found one particular list of recipients of HLF aid (via the Islamic Relief Agency) on which families received much larger sums "than the amounts allocated by [HLF and the Islamic Relief Agency] to families included on other lists." Twenty-five of the twenty-eight families on the list "were families of Hamas activists who were killed, arrested or deported." The Court concluded that "[HLF], through the help of [the Islamic Relief Agency], is supporting with significant amounts of money especially those families of Hamas activists. . . . From this the conclusion was established that the main purpose of [the HLF] and of [the Islamic Relief Agency] is to provide massive support to Hamas."[21]

*　　*　　*

Equally important to HLF's fund-raising, however, is IAP's political work and organizing. The Islamic Association for Palestine (IAP) was founded in 1981 in Chicago, Illinois. Ever since Hamas was formed, six years later in 1987, IAP has served as its primary voice within the United States. It was at an IAP conference in 1989 that this book's opening vignette occurred, with the veiled Hamas commander lauding the terrorist acts of Hamas and praising the history of armed resistance against the Jews and the Israelis in the Middle East.[22]

At that conference, a prominent sign on the dais read "Islamic Resistance Movement—Hamas: The Pioneer in the Jihad Path in Palestine." Speaker after speaker came to the podium and spread the word of Hamas. Finally, Sheikh Muharram al-Aarifi led the gathering in a chant whose basic premise was to exalt Hamas as the movement of everyone in the room and as the voice of jihad "against the monkeys," i.e., the Jews and the Israelis.

The IAP has consistently denied that it has supported Hamas in any form. In an interview that I conducted with Mohammad al-Hassan at the IAP's headquarters in Richardson, Texas, in preparation for the airing of "Jihad in America" in 1994, I asked Mr. al-Hassan whether IAP supported the Hamas point of view. He responded, "Not as, the Hamas point of view, no. [IAP] supports liberation of Palestine, [IAP] supports informing the public about the Palestinian issue, [IAP] supports informing the public about the different groups, the different activities which are going on in Palestine. But [IAP] doesn't take a position in support of any one group per se."[23] Today little has changed. The IAP routinely issues denials that the organization is in any way affiliated with or supportive of Hamas.

Yet the IAP has printed and disseminated the Hamas charter in its original Arabic ever since 1988. An address that appears on many copies is that of a post office in Tucson, Arizona, where the

IAP Information Office was located before it moved to the suburbs of Dallas. Furthermore, IAP has printed many communiqués and other announcements by Hamas. In the November/December 1989 issue of the IAP's Arabic-language magazine *Ila Filistin*, a full-page advertisement featured the following proclamation: "The only way to liberate Palestine, all Palestine, is by way of Jihad, and any other way except Jihad will only lead to strengthen [*sic*] the Zionist occupation." This claim was closely followed by the declaration that "the Islamic Resistance Movement (Hamas) is the conscience of the Palestinian people, and it is the hope against all those who betrayed and those who are against the Palestinian issue." At the end were instructions to send donations for jihad for the sake of Allah to the Occupied Land Fund.[24]

In the years since the founding of Hamas, the IAP's audiovisual arm, Aqsa Vision, has distributed numerous videotapes lauding the activities of Hamas and even portraying training exercises for actual Hamas terrorists. One such video, entitled "Izz al-Din al-Qassem Brigades," subtitled "Gaza, September 1992," includes footage of Hamas terrorists carrying automatic weapons and jumping out of trees. In addition, it includes interviews with Hamas terrorists who are preparing to be martyred for their cause. At the end the screen shows the Aqsa Vision name and phone number. The latter is that of the Islamic Association for Palestine's office in Richardson, Texas. Other videos have been distributed showing the conditions of the deportation of over 400 Hamas and Palestinian Islamic Jihad leaders from Israel and the Occupied Territories to Lebanon in 1992. All of these videos are intended to evoke sympathy for Hamas members, despite the fact that

Hamas's agenda includes the destruction of the State of Israel through terrorist acts.

The IAP's primary activity has been its annual conferences. At the Kansas City conference in 1989, in addition to the Hamas commander, one speaker was Yusuf al-Qaradawi, an Egyptian-born religious scholar based in Qatar who created a stir in France with the publication of his book *The Lawful and the Prohibited in Islam.* (In it, al-Qaradawi wrote that a husband is entitled to beat his wife if she does not oblige him with "obedience and cooperation.")[25] "Palestine cannot be liberated except by Islam!" al-Qaradawi told his IAP audience. "So, if they fight us with Judaism, we will fight them with Islam! If they fight with the Torah, we will fight them with the Koran. . . . If they say their temple, we have the Masjid al-Aqsa. . . . On the Hour of Judgment, the Muslims will fight the Jews and kill them, until the Jews will hide behind the stone, and the stone and the tree will say, O Servant of Allah, O Muslim! There is a Jew behind me, come and kill him. . . . Muslims will not be victorious by nationalism, and not by monarchy, and not by democracy, and not by Marxism—they will only be victorious by Islam."[26]

Another incendiary speech was given by Sheikh Ahmed al-Qattan, a Palestinian cleric based in Kuwait: "Greetings to those who shoot at the Jews with the catapult, and to those who poke out the eyes of the Jews with the slingshot. . . . In 1967 . . . the Jews sang, "Muhammad is dead and he gave birth to girls . . . [and we answer,] "O sons of pigs and monkeys, Muhammad is not dead and he did not give birth to girls. Rather, *khaybar, khaybar* [death] to Jews; Muhammad's Army will return!"[27]

During the Gulf War, the IAP organized an emergency conference in response to the American troop buildup in Saudi Arabia. The participants issued a resolution condemning "the American crusades." Khalil al-Qawka, a Hamas leader from Palestine, wanted to go further:

> Today, America is right here at your doorstep, in everybody's house. Ba'al, the idol, is back and stands erect in the Arabian Peninsula. Is there a Muhammad to slay the Ba'al of our times? . . . The Marines, dear brothers, are stealing the doors of your houses, and the doors of your mosques, in obstinate and open provocation. They are at our doors. Their plan is to penetrate the flesh of our girls. And our honor, and our values, in order to turn our society into a perverted nation.[28]

Later, a choir of eight- and nine-year-old children sang revolutionary Islamic songs praising Hamas. In syncopated rhythm, they imitated Hamas knife-stabbings.

The IAP's 1996 and 1997 conferences held in Chicago featured not only militant Islamic leaders and repeated exhortations to support terrorist attacks, but also condemnations of the United States. The former was typified by Mohammad abu Faris, a Jordanian Islamic leader: "We were blamed in writing that we do not comply with what our religion orders us to. It orders us to fight the Jews and we did not kill them, and [by that omission] we did not perform our religion [religious duty]. Therefore, had we claimed that we do perform what our religion orders us and obliges us to do while we are not doing it—then they [those who have blamed us] would have been right. They wrote that our reality contradicts our religion."[29] Furthermore, abu Faris stated, "There is only one way to liberate Palestine and Al-Aqsa, and that is the fighting, that is the Jihad, that is the slaughtering, that is the butchering . . . call it dialogue." At the conclusion of his statement, the assembled crowd erupted in laughter at the mention of any type of "dialogue."

The latter was typified by Abdulrahman Alamoudi, who at the time of his speech before the 1996 IAP annual convention in Chicago was the executive director of the American Muslim Council (AMC) and a politically active member of the Muslim community within the United States. Alamoudi did not advocate violence against the United States, at least not openly: "if we are outside this country we can say O Allah, destroy America, but once we are here, our mission in this country is to change it. . . . There is no way for Muslims to be violent in America, no way. We have other means . . . to do it. You can be violent anywhere else but in America."[30] His message was surely not lost on his listeners.

The 1997 IAP Annual Conference attracted several thousand Muslims for three days of militant lectures focused on Palestine, Islam, Israel, and Jews. Featured speakers included an impressive array of Hamas supporters from the Islamic Action Front (IAF) in Jordan, as well as a number of prominent militant American Muslim leaders. Speakers delivered lectures in English and Arabic on panels with titles such as: "Zionism: A Racist and Colonial Ideology," "Contemporary Movements of Islamic Renewal and the Societal Plan," "The Settlement Process in the Middle East: Results and Expectations," "The Dome of the Rock: the First *Qibla* [Muslim direction of prayer] or the Eternal Capital of the Jews?" Lectures varied in their level of militancy and vitriol toward Jews, with the Arabic lectures being decidedly more militant. One presenter was Jordan's Ahmed al-Kufahi, a member of the Islamic Action Front (IAF) political party. The IAF serves as the political voice of the Muslim Brotherhood movement in Jordan. At the conference, al-Kufahi commented on the obligation of engaging in jihad on behalf of the land of Palestine:

> In Islam, if your enemy occupies a small piece of your land, then you have to declare jihad against the enemy. Jihad becomes a must and a religious obligation on all Muslims to go and fight the enemy. . . . women must go for jihad without taking permission from their husbands . . . slaves without taking permission from their masters . . . boys without taking permission from their fathers. . . . Palestine is occupied by the enemy. The occupation of Palestine shouldn't be dealt with as a regional one [issue] but as an Islamic obligation, because occupation of any Islamic land is a violation to the Sovereignty of Islamic world.[31]

Ali al-Bayanuni, leader of the Syrian branch of the Muslim Brotherhood, added, "The Palestine issue is the most important issue for Muslims and its liberation and confronting the Zionist challenge should be on the top of our priorities as Muslims, and we should prepare ourselves for that task. Jihad is an Islamic obligation and a must on all Muslims."[32]

Year after year, the rhetoric has continued. At the 1999 IAP Annual Conference in Chicago, Salah Sultan, who delivered the Friday prayer sermon, set the tone by indicating that American support of Israel would come back to haunt the United States: "My advice to the American society: See the realities, do not take them from the false media that bank on your credulity and submissiveness. The Zionist regime is a danger to the Jews, a danger to Christians, a danger to Americans."[33] Sultan also encouraged the youth at the conference to strive toward martyrdom for Palestine by saying, "I want every child to sleep on the wound of Palestine and the actions of martyrdom, just like that mother in the country whose son wrote to her that they are to meet in Paradise. . . ."

Blatant anti-Semitic rhetoric spewed from another session at which the Jordanian Sheikh Ahmed al-Kufahi stated, "Jews are the enemies of humanity even before they are the enemies of Muslims, therefore it is necessary to remove them from power."

As recently as the 2000 IAP Annual Conference, convened in Chicago over Thanksgiving weekend, fund-raising for Hamas was on full display. Imam Jamal Said from Bridgeview, Illinois, put it like this:

> I appeal to you, on this night that is ushering in the holy month of Ramadan, to be generous and give plenty, to keep the light in the houses of our martyrs burning. We have boxes here that say "Help us, help the Aqsa cause, Islamic Association for Palestine!" We want you to fill those boxes. There is no better charity than to pay for the family of a martyr.[34]

Renowned Kuwaiti sheikh Tariq Suweidan added incendiary comments for his rapt audience: "Palestine will not be liberated but through jihad. Nothing can be achieved without sacrificing blood. The Jews will meet their end at our hands."[35]

A fund-raising session was held to raise $200,000 for the Islamic Association for Palestine. As an impetus for giving to the organization, the fund-raiser read aloud the Arabic will of "martyr" Hamdi Yasin, who died while killing an Israeli officer by driving his car into a military checkpoint.

> I say, it is not correct when some people say that we commit suicide because we do not value life. We love life, but life in dignity. . . . I cannot allow God's houses to be violated without defending them. . . . At the Law Faculty of Al-Azhar University I was about to receive a certificate in law, but in this phase I prefer another kind of certificate, the other life, martyrdom in the path of God, the other certificate is martyrdom in the path of God. There is a big difference between the two certificates. . . . *Finally I pray to Almighty God that my action may result in the death of the greatest number of God's enemies possible.* Let them know that our hallowed places, and our brains, and our blood are not cheap. I profess that there is no god but the One God, and that Muhammad is the messenger of God. [emphasis added][36]

There are other means by which IAP spreads its violent, pro-Hamas rhetoric. One avenue of expression has been the use of an

Internet e-mail list which provides news from "Palestine" and press releases from the IAP. In May 2000, IAP president Rafiq Jaber wrote in one of these e-mail postings that the Palestinian Authority must recognize that the only means to deal with the Israelis is through violence. Lauding the success of the Hizballah terrorist organization in prompting an Israeli withdrawal from southern Lebanon, Jaber wrote, "Maybe the PA [Palestinian Authority] will take a hard look at the slippery road it is now traveling and join the resistance to Zionist occupation in order to liberate the land of Palestine. I firmly believe that Palestine will never be liberated by any other means." [37]

On August 28, 2000, IAP distributed a Hamas communiqué on its e-mail bulletin that praised the Hamas terrorist mujahid Mahmoud abu Hannoud for killing Israelis. It stated, "He was able, all praises to Allah, to kill three enemy soldiers and wound nine others, one of whom sustained serious injuries." [38]

Another avenue of expression for the IAP has been through its publications. The IAP currently publishes a biweekly newspaper called *Al-Zaitonah* which, like its now defunct English-language counterpart the *Muslim World Monitor,* celebrates successful Hamas terrorist attacks. In 1994 one headline proclaimed: "In its greatest operation, Hamas takes credit for the bombing of an Israeli bus in the center of Tel Aviv." Other articles warn of "anti-Muslim conspiracies," for example by denouncing the first World Trade Center bombing as a Mossad-FBI plot (designed, of course, to discredit Islam). Sometimes, IAP simply republishes extremist articles from the right-wing Liberty Lobby plus a stable of left-wing conspiracy theorists. More recently, articles have run in which different organizations have competed for credit in promoting Hamas in the political arena. In one interview in *Al-Zaitonah*, Abdulrahman Alamoudi, the former executive director of the American Muslim Council (AMC), stated, "I request the brothers [in the IAP] not to demand too much from us in terms of Palestine. Our position with regard to the peace process is well-known. We are the ones who went to the White House and defended what is called Hamas." [39]

Across the IAP's many venues, explicit references to Hamas have dwindled since antiterrorism legislation prohibited the provision of material support or resources to Hamas from the United States. But the lack of mention of Hamas has made little difference in practice. Raeed Tayeh, an IAP representative, explained the organization's agenda at a rally held at Lafayette Park in Washington, D.C., on October 28, 2000:

> I come with three messages that the Islamic Association for Palestine would like to reiterate. I am going to say them in Arabic and then in English. Number one: *kul philastin min Nahar il al-Bahar*, all of Palestine from the Jordan River to the Mediterranean Sea. Number two: *Kul Philastin Quds*, all Palestine is sacred, not just just al-Quds, and number three, *Aqsa al alahi eluhum*, our *Aqsa* is not their temple.

*　　*　　*

The FBI believes that Hamas has even gone so far as to set up a for-profit American corporation. On September 5, 2001, agents from the Joint Terrorism Task Force operating out of Dallas, Texas, executed a search warrant against InfoCom Corporation, an Internet service provider in Richardson, Texas, for its ties to Hamas. Though the affadavit requesting approval for the search of InfoCom's offices remains classified, the Office of Foreign Assets Control (OFAC) notified InfoCom that two of its bank accounts, totaling $70,000, had been frozen due to a lump-sum investment of $250,000 provided to InfoCom in 1993 by Nadia Elashi Marzook, the wife of Musa abu Marzook.[40] As a by-product of the search instituted against InfoCom, the Bureau of Export Administration had suspended InfoCom's export privileges based on suspicions that InfoCom had violated U.S. export control laws by making shipments to Libya and Iran, two states listed as state sponsors of terrorism.[41] Furthermore, subpoenas were served on two of InfoCom's clients, the Islamic Association for Palestine and the Holy Land Foundation for Relief and Development. Ghassan Dahduli, a former employee of InfoCom and an officer in the American Middle Eastern League for Palestine (AMELP)—a 501(c)(3) charity with direct links to the Islamic Association for Palestine—was taken into custody by federal authorities on September 22, 2001, after refusing to answer questions.[42] Dahduli has also been implicated as an associate of one of the individuals who was convicted for a role in the August 1998 attacks on the United States embassies in Africa.

InfoCom hosted the Web sites of more than 500 companies and nonprofit groups, including a variety of Islamic groups and charities, including the Holy Land Foundation. Rafiq Jaber, president of the Islamic Association for Palestine, scoffed that InfoCom was "being raided because it's a Muslim company, like the Holy Land Foundation."[43]

Was InfoCom really just an internet service provider? Or was it providing "material support" for Hamas? Was it involved in technology transfers to terrorist-supporting regimes? It is important to stress that InfoCom has not been convicted of any wrongdoing—yet the confluence of location (Richardson) and personnel (Dahduli and the Marzooks) are troubling.

With technology, publications, fund-raising, and recruiting, Hamas does it all in the United States. Of course, it is still highly active in the Middle East, and it will always target Israelis as its highest priority for actual operations. But as confrontation with the West heats up, Hamas operatives are ready to turn their formidable apparatus against American targets.

Furthermore, some evidence suggests that Hamas has coordinated with other groups here in the United States. Leaders of the Palestinian Islamic Jihad have spoken of efforts to coordinate with their "brothers" in Hamas (see Chapter 6). Gatherings of multiple groups have helped reinforce their mutual interests.

Consider the statements of one particular Iranian-American imam, Muhammad al-Asi: "Let me say that Hamas, the [Palestinian] Islamic Jihad, and the Islamic Resistance in the Occupied Lands are part of a general Islamic revitalization, political-military reinstatement in the arena of the world, that is not confined to the Occupied Lands and that strictly belongs to the general Islamic condition throughout the world."[44] He has even gone so far as to say that if Muslims in the United States are not able to take time off to volunteer with these organizations, then they need to "establish contact with these groups and see what aid they want from the U.S."[45]

Al-Asi is a controversial figure. He was previously the imam of the Muslim Community School in Potomac, Maryland[46] and the director of the Islamic Education Center there.[47] At one time he was the imam of the Islamic Center in Washington, D.C., but in 1983 he was forced out; nonetheless he still preaches on the sidewalk outside on Fridays. The Islamic Education Center in Potomac has received substantial funding in the past by the Alavi Foundation, which the FBI claims is "entirely controlled by the government of Iran."[48] According to an article in the December 1995 edition of *The American Spectator,* the Islamic Education Center in Potomac "offers Farsi-language primary school classes that are fully accredited with the Iranian national educational system. It also offers religious education classes for adults and children, and distributes Iranian government prop-aganda. At the center's bookstore, interested parties can purchase the original version of Khomeini's *fatwa*—or religious order—condemning British author Salman Rushdie to death for having blasphemed against Islam. The *fatwa* instructs Muslims through-out the world that it is a 'religious duty' to assassinate Rushdie. The bookstore also sells videotaped speeches by anti-Semitic fanatics such as the Swiss-based Ahmed Huber, who extols Aya-tollah Khomeini as the living continuation of Adolf Hitler." In short, al-Asi is strongly pro-Iranian, yet that has not stopped him from praising Hamas and linking up with other organi-zations.

Al-Asi has been present at a number of radical Islamic

conferences through the years including those held on behalf of the Islamic Committee for Palestine, where he made incendiary statements regarding striking at American interests worldwide ("If the Americans are placing their forces in the Persian Gulf, we should be creating another war front for the Americans in the Muslim World, and specifically where American interests are concentrated—in Egypt, in Turkey, in the Indian subcontinent, just to mention a few. Strike at American interests there!"). When the United Association for Studies and Research convened a conference including radicals from groups ranging from Hamas to Hizballah to the Algerian Islamic Salvation Front, al-Asi appeared and gave a presentation on the issue of "The Islamic Movement and the Need for a Comprehensive Political and Intellectual Organization."[49] He has also appeared at conferences of the Islamic Association for Palestine. Al-Asi has even been hosted by the Islamic Republic of Iran; on January 30, 1990, he was hosted by Ayatollah Khamene'i, the religious leader in Iran who succeeded the Ayatollah Khomeini after he died.[50]

* * *

In meeting after meeting here in the United States, the same people and organizations mix and match. Through some people, connections are forged with Iran; through others, with Osama bin Laden; through others, with countries like Sudan. America's role in facilitating these connections is more than peripheral.

Having looked at a single organization with several American tentacles, it may be helpful to next flip the microscope around, and look at a single tentacle of a different organization. Perhaps the most disturbing story of American terrorist infiltration is the story of one unusual tentacle that reached its way into the University of South Florida in Tampa.

Chapter Six

JIHAD IN THE ACADEMY

ON A FORMER SANDY AIRSTRIP near Tampa sits a remarkable, very contemporary Sun Belt college campus. The University of South Florida, founded with only 2,000 students in 1960, has grown rapidly during its short four-decade life. With branches in St. Petersburg, Sarasota-Manatee, and Lakeland, it now sprawls across 164 buildings and boasts an enrollment of 37,000. While drawing students from far and wide, its main constituency is from the Tampa region, including many Latinos.

Few large urban universities are as academically competitive. The average SAT score of entering freshmen hovers around 1100. The university's graduate programs are broad and deep, including specialties in medicine and biotech. Meanwhile, the Tampa area has emerged as a top southern hi-tech center, with many entrepreneurial ventures growing out of town-gown relationships in the familiar pattern of Stanford in Silicon Valley or M.I.T. in Cambridge. On its Web site, the university calls itself "one of the great legacies of the watershed social and intellectual developments of mid-twentieth century America."[1]

Unfortunately, the University of South Florida has also been a center of the American jihad movement.

It all began innocently enough. In 1989, on narrow, dead-end 130th Street, a sign was affixed to the last house on the block memorializing "Izz al-Din al-Qassam . . . [who] declared Jihad against the British and Zionist invasion of Palestine. He was martyred on November 19, 1935 in Yabrod, Palestine. Al-Qassam has become a symbol of heroism, resistance, occupation, and invasion of steadfast Palestine." In fact, al-Qassam may be the most exalted figure in recent Palestinian history. As noted by scholar Ziad abu-Amr, he is "the main source of inspiration for the Islamic Jihad movement. Al-Qassam is considered the movement's first pioneer. He is viewed as the first leader of the Palestinian armed resistance in the history of modern Palestine and the true father of the armed Palestinian revolution."[2] The Tampa house—being used as a mosque—was named by USF professor Sami al-Arian.

To find a mosque similarly memorialized you would have to go to the Gaza Strip. There the al-Qassam Mosque is a recognized hangout for the Palestinian Islamic Jihad, a terrorist organization that has established as its trademark the decapitating and dismembering of both Jews and Palestinian "collaborators." Islamic Jihad is not just at war with Israel. The movement sees Israel's existence as part of a larger American-directed plot against Islam. According to abu-Amr, the Palestinian Islamic Jihad sees Israel and America "as two faces of the same coin."[3]

From 1991 to 1995 one of the world's most lethal terrorist factions used a think tank affiliated with the University of South Florida (along with a separate nonprofit organization) as a base for some of its top leaders. The formula was simple: use the laws, freedoms, and loopholes of the most liberal nation on earth to help finance and direct one of the most violent international terrorism groups in the world.

At the center of it all was Sami al-Arian. A Palestinian professor of engineering, al-Arian came to USF in 1986 to teach that subject along with computer science. One of his first undertakings was to incorporate the Islamic Concern Project, soon to be renamed the Islamic Committee for Palestine. The ICP's ostensible purposes were "charitable, cultural, social, educational and religious in which the concept of brotherhood, freedom, justice, unity, piety, righteousness and peace shall be propagated."[4] Al-Arian and his brother-in-law Mazen al-Najjar were among the founding members of ICP's Board of Directors.

Al-Arian was also the chairman of the board of another nonprofit organization, the World and Islam Studies Enterprise (WISE), a think-tank organized "exclusively for educational and academic research and analysis, and promotion of international peace and understanding."[5] On March 11, 1992, WISE entered into a formal agreement with the University of South Florida outlining a series of cooperative programs for research and graduate-student enrichment, all in the name of "multiculturalism." Together, the university and WISE would cohost forums, sponsor USF graduate students, and share resources.

When I interviewed al-Arian in the early 1990s, the soft-spoken professor denied that either ICP or WISE had any connection to the Palestinian Islamic Jihad. Rather than being "political," he said, ICP was a "charitable, social, and cultural type group." When I asked him who al-Qassam was, he shrugged, "A Muslim scholar." [6] Yet, as I first showed with videotaped evidence in "Jihad in America," the ICP was already acting as a support group for the Palestinian Islamic Jihad. The connections between the ICP, WISE, and the University of South Florida would only grow more intertwined as the 1990s progressed.

The ICP and WISE were almost identical organizations. For fifteen months both shared office space and a post office box secured by al-Arian in 1994.[7] Even more significant was the match-up in leadership. Al-Arian, Bashir Nafi, Mazen al-Najjar, and Khalil Shikaki were all executive members of both organizations. Shikaki, one of the first directors of WISE, was also the brother of Fathi Shikaki, secretary-general of the Palestinian Islamic Jihad. Khalil negotiated the agreement between WISE and the university. Another member of the circle was Ramadan Abdullah Shallah, who served as director of administration of WISE and was a member of the Board of Directors of ICP while also employed as an adjunct professor in Middle Eastern studies at USF. Shallah taught a course on Middle Eastern politics that attracted some student criticisms because he referred to Israel only as "Palestine." [8]

For legal purposes, however, ICP had no connection to the university. Thus it was on his own time that Professor al-Arian edited *Inquiry*, the official ICP magazine. *Inquiry* routinely ran incendiary attacks on Jews and the United States. One article, for example, argued, "The mistake of the Jews of today who occupy Palestine was made as well by the Roman aggressors of 933 A.D. . . . [It] is to underestimate the faith in Allah of our people in resisting all forms of evil, tyranny and aggression. Our Jihad is the greatest weapon we have which no nation or Zionist can take away. It is greater than the Japanese suicide *kamikaze* missions for ours is for Allah and He is great."

Inquiry also carried many articles about the Palestinian Islamic Jihad. In January 1993, the magazine ran a full-length interview with PIJ secretary-general Fathi Shikaki, the brother of its board member. "The movement considers itself an independent, Islamic, and popular movement with Islam as its ideology, grassroots popular action and armed struggle as its means, and the liberation of Palestine as its objective," Shikaki told *Inquiry*.[9] To this day, a copy of this interview can be found on the Palestinian Islamic Jihad's Web site.[10] When Paul Eedle, Reuters' Egyptian bureau chief, went to Damascus to interview Shikaki in 1993, the secretary-general gave him a copy of the *Inquiry* article as background information.[11]

In addition to *Inquiry*, the ICP also published two Arabic-language publications, *Al-Islam wa-Filistin (Islam and Palestine)* and *Al-Mujahid*.[12] *Islam and Palestine* served as a medium for Palestinian Islamic Jihad communiqués. These broadsides regularly glorified the Palestinian Islamic Jihad's terrorist attacks against Israel and celebrated the murder of Palestinians accused of collaborating with the State of Israel. In the October 3, 1990, issue of the Arabic-language magazine *Al-Liwa*, Fathi Shikaki was quoted as saying that *Islam and Palestine* was the most recent in a line of magazines issued by the Palestinian Islamic Jihad.[13] *Islam and Palestine* proudly reprinted the interview on November 8, 1990.

On September 1, 1988, *Islam and Palestine* published a special edition entitled "The Holy Warrior [*Mujahid*] Facing Interrogation and Torture." The article explained that jihad was a long-term struggle: "[T]he war of Islam against the *kufar* [infidels] and the war of the *ummah* [community] against the Jewish land in Palestine won't happen in a single attack, but it will be a long and arduous process of struggle. A long line of buried *mujahideen* will make it possible for the Islamic *ummah* to have the power for victory. If the *ummah* wants this power, then there is only one way, the *jihad* way, following *La Illah illallah* (There is no god but Allah). This will happen through martyrdom struggles, or by torture, or by imprisonment, or by deportation, or by embargoes." The ICP's contact address in Tampa appeared on the same page. The ICP's second Arabic-language magazine, *Al-Mujahid,* was much less secretive about its connections with Islamic Jihad.[14] The Palestinian Islamic Jihad logo appeared on the front page of each edition, along with the following words: "Publication Produced by the Islamic Jihad Movement in Palestine—Lebanon."

When I interviewed al-Arian in 1994, he claimed that he was never connected with the ICP when *Islam and Palestine* was being published. He insisted that *Islam and Palestine* ceased publication around 1989 and that he only took over the ICP in 1990.[15] Yet *Islam and Palestine* was published until 1992. Furthermore, on each issue from1988 through 1992, the addresses listed for subscriptions and letters to the editor pointed straight to Tampa:

ICP
P.O. Box 350256
Tampa, Florida 33695 USA [for issues spanning from April 1, 1988 through August 1, 1989]

Or

ICP
P.O. Box 82009
Tampa, Florida 33682–2009 USA [for issues spanning from September 1, 1989 through December 1992].

While disseminating the Palestinian Islamic Jihad's newsletters, the ICP was also organizing annual conventions in cities across the United States, including Chicago, St. Louis, and Cleveland. In reviewing more than forty hours of recordings from five major conferences, we found that the ICP:

- brought militant Islamic terrorist leaders into the United States from all over the world, including Sheikh Omar Abdel Rahman and representatives of Hizballah, the Sudanese National Islamic Front, the Tunisian An-Nahda, Hamas, and Lebanon's Tawheed;
- raised money for Islamic Jihad charities and other terrorist-associated organizations and tax-exempt foundations; and

- made overt calls for terrorist acts against Israeli, Egyptian, Tunisian, Algerian, and American targets.

The rhetoric was lurid and incendiary. At one 1991 rally, al-Arian warmed up the crowd of three hundred supporters with calls for jihad and "Death to Israel."[16] The guest of honor was Sheikh Abdel Aziz Odeh, spiritual leader of the Islamic Jihad, who helped raise thousands of dollars for the cause. (Evidence uncovered at the first World Trade Center bombing trials indicated that Sheikh Aziz Odeh met followers of Sheikh Abdel Rahman at New York's John F. Kennedy International Airport prior to that bomb blast to discuss terrorist acts on American soil. Even today, Odeh remains an unindicted coconspirator in that deadly attack.)

Tape recordings of ICP conferences show that funds were solicited for the explicit purpose of "sponsoring martyrs." At a Chicago conference held in 1990, one speaker enumerated the "operations" (i.e., terrorist attacks carried out by Islamic Jihad martyrs). "We are giving you a list of sixteen martyrs," says the speaker. "Some of these died in amphibious operations. Some died in assault operations. The families need your assistance. Each martyr needs one thousand dollars. Is there someone here to sponsor ten martyrs?"[17]

Six months after my 1994 documentary "Jihad in America" identified the ICP as a fundraiser for Islamic Jihad, Michael Fechter of the *Tampa Tribune* wrote a trail-blazing two-part frontpage series exposing ICP and WISE's connections with terrorist groups:

On the University of Florida campus, Sami al-Arian is an award-winning young engineering professor.

In his off hours, he presided over a nonprofit organization that helps raise money in the name of two groups that claim responsibility for bombings that have killed hundreds in Israel and around the world. . . .

Al-Arian refused requests for a face-to-face interview, but did answer some questions over the telephone. He asked for questions in writing but did not respond to a registered letter.

In the limited interview with the Tampa Tribune, al-Arian discussed one of the Islamic Jihad's and Hamas' tactics, the suicide bomb. "When people have nowhere else to go, (when) they are being humiliated day in and day out . . . This is not an irrational act," he said.

The series set off a huge controversy at USF. Islamic critics charged the *Tampa Tribune* with "persecuting" Muslims. Fechter was falsely accused of distorting the news. Nonetheless, two weeks after the *Tribune*'s reports, the university suspended its relationship with WISE.

Then five months later, on October 26, 1995, a bomb exploded in Malta that soon reverberated all over southern Florida. Dr. Fathi Shikaki, the secretary-general of the Palestinian Islamic Jihad, was assassinated. His murder was almost certainly committed by Israel's Mossad. One week later, Shikaki's body was greeted at Damascus Airport by a full military honor guard. Standing directly beside the body, in his new position as secretary-general of the Palestinian Islamic Jihad, was none other than Ramadan Abdullah Shallah, former adjunct professor of Middle Eastern Studies at the University of South Florida.

Shallah's connections to the Palestinian Islamic Jihad ran right back to its origins in Egypt in the 1970s. Indeed, present at the creation were no fewer than three men who would come to be affiliated with the University of South Florida through WISE. At the beginning, the Palestinian Islamic Jihad was an offshoot of the militant Islamic group the Muslim Brotherhood, based in Egypt.[18] Whereas the Brotherhood had focused on jihad against Egypt's secular government, some Palestinian members wanted to direct their efforts toward the Occupied Territories of Palestine.[19] Among these original founders of the PIJ were Fathi Shikaki, Abdel Aziz Odeh, Bashir Nafi,[20] and Ramadan Abdullah Shallah[21]— all, with the exception of Fathi Shikaki, later associated with ICP and WISE.

Shallah migrated to England in 1986,[22] joining Palestinian Islamic Jihad activist Bashir Nafi,[23] who had moved to London in 1983.[24] Together, they organized communications between the Palestinian Islamic Jihad's leaders and operatives in the Middle East. Their primary contact within the Occupied Territories was Omar Shallah, Ramadan Shallah's brother.[25] At the same time Shallah and Nafi operated their London outpost,[26] they were also associated with WISE and ICP.[27] Nafi has been called a "leading ideologue" of the Islamic Jihad movement.[28] Khalil Shikaki has said that Nafi was the person who recruited him to join WISE.

Although he became WISE's director of research, Nafi was no ordinary scholar. While in England he wrote for Islamist publications in France and London, including *Falastin al-Muslimah*, the monthly magazine of Hamas, *al-Hilal ad-Dawli*, and *at-Taliyah al-Islamiyah*. Although one of the oldest members of the Palestinian Islamic Jihad, Nafi was *not* considered as a successor to the murdered Fathi Shikaki, according to reports in the Jordanian newspaper *Al-Urdun*. In June 1996, Nafi was arrested by INS agents in Herndon, Virginia, outside the offices of the International Institute of Islamic Thought (IIIT), a nonprofit institute sponsored by the S.A.A.R. Foundation, a billion-dollar Saudi conglomerate. (S.A.A.R. also funded ICP and WISE.) Nafi, who was employed by IIIT at the time of his arrest, was charged with violating his visa, which stipulated that WISE would be his sole employer in the United States. He was deported.

Needless to say, the revelation that the new leader of one of the world's most notorious terror organizations was also a University of South Florida faculty member caused a great deal of commotion in Tampa. To that point, the *Tampa Tribune* series and my "Jihad in America" documentary had been severely criticized. Sami al-Arian had claimed to know nothing about his protégé's terrorist background. Yet as Carnot Nelson, a psychology professor, now argued, "What [Shallah's departure] does is validate everything Steven Emerson has been saying." Not all university officials agreed. "There may be a terrorist element to [the Islamic Jihad]," said Harry Bratton, university vice president, "but it is also an important cultural group in the Middle East." Bratton went on to say that critics were making an invalid "assumption that because [Shallah] was elevated to head an organization that has a terrorist element . . . he has terrorism on his mind." [29]

The university's official response was to commission an investigation and report from William Reece Smith, a prominent Tampa attorney and former provost of the university. At a cost of nearly $20,000, Smith interviewed many people and wrote up a 98-page analysis that largely absolved the university of blame. Noting that WISE was involved in some legitimate scholarly activities, and that the university had neither the time nor the resources to investigate every organization with which it might affiliate, his criticism was muted: "I do find it unusual that committee members did not ask, out of curiosity if nothing else, some rather basic questions which would have identified the officers of WISE. There, I think, it failed to act as one might reasonably expect." [30]

Elsewhere, the news of Shallah's new position was not well received—especially among military officers at MacDill Air Force Base, near Tampa. On two previous occasions, Shallah had been invited to brief U.S. Central Command (Centcom) there.

The revelation of Palestinian Islamic Jihad activities in Tampa led to a federal investigation. FBI officials were soon scouring the records of the ICP, WISE, and its members. In November 1995, two Florida bank accounts totaling some $17,000 and belonging to Ramadan Abdullah Shallah were frozen under a Presidential order. On Monday, November 20, 1995, federal officials searched the campus offices and home of al-Arian under a warrant for evidence of perjury and immigration-related infractions. In an affidavit filed in support of the government's warrant petition, the INS charged that on applying for citizenship in the United States, al-Arian had failed to list organizations to which he belonged prior to his arrival and during his residence in the United States. Although listing the Islamic Society of North America, the Islamic Community of Tampa, the IEEE (the Institute for Electrical and Electronics Engineers), and the IEEE Computer Society, al-Arian had failed to mention either the ICP or WISE, even though he was a founding officer of both.[31] The affidavit further stated that al-Arian had placed "numerous" phone calls from his ICP office to the Iranian Interest Section (the equivalent of an embassy) in the United States and to the Sudanese Embassy—despite the fact that both nations are on the official State Department list of nations supporting international terrorism. They also found that al-Arian had made a series of calls to Siraj El-din Yousif, a Sudanese diplomatic operative in New York who was later implicated in and expelled for participating in the Day of Terror bombing plot in New York in 1993.

In executing the search warrants, federal authorities uncovered one of the largest collections of terrorist fund-raising and propaganda material ever seized in the United States. According to federal sources, both WISE and ICP had extensive financial and political ties with Islamic extremists worldwide. Sheikh Omar Abdel Rahman had been a guest speaker at one ICP conference.

In a follow-up affidavit, FBI Special Agent Barry Carmody reported the discovery of a particularly damning document: "Located and seized at the residence of Sami al-Arian on November 20, 1995, was a letter written by Sami al-Arian in which al-Arian is soliciting funds for the Islamic movement in Palestine. . . . This letter also appeals for support for the Jihad so that the people will not lose faith in Islam . . . [T]he Jihad has been declared an international terrorist organization by the Department of State." [32]

The complete contents of this letter were not revealed until the letter was declassified in October 2000. Al-Arian's letter had been written to a Kuwaiti citizen, soliciting funds on behalf of the Palestinian Islamic Jihad. [33] In it, al-Arian describes an "operation" that needs to be emulated by the movement. It appears that the "operation" was the dual suicide bombings by Palestinian Islamic Jihad terrorists at the Beit Lid bus junction in Israel that resulted in the deaths of nineteen Israelis. Al-Arian also described the relations between the PIJ and Hamas as having improved: "The link with the brothers in Hamas is very good and making steady progress, and there are serious attempts at unification and permanent coordination." [34]

By the late 1990s, a great deal of information about the ICP, WISE, and the Palestinian Islamic Jihad had come to light. It was known that Tarik Hamdi, one of WISE's board members, personally delivered a satellite telephone and battery pack to Osama bin Laden in Afghanistan in May 1998. The FBI had also seized correspondence between Ramadan Shallah and Khalil Shikaki showing that Shallah had served as a contact person for messages between the two Shikaki brothers prior to Fathi Shikaki's assassination. One letter, for example, showed that Shallah was involved in the governing of the Palestinian Islamic Jihad even while he was in Tampa and that he used Khalil Shikaki as a resource to further the education of one of the organization's terrorist leaders. In the letter, Shallah relayed Fathi Shikaki's request for assistance from Khalil to procure an academic recommendation for a student living in Damascus named Anwar Abdel Hadi Mohammad abu Taha. According to the June 1999 issue of the *Middle East Intelligence Bulletin,* Anwar Abu Taha is the "chief of [the Palestinian Islamic Jihad's] military wing."

Despite all this evidence, the ICP and WISE leaders have faced few legal consequences. For a time, Mazen al-Najjar, the USF faculty member who ran day-to-day operations at WISE, was taken into custody. Al-Najjar was brought up on visa violations and immigration-fraud charges, including perpetrating a fictitious marriage to an American citizen on the sole grounds of obtaining permanent resident status in the United States. In an immigration hearing held in July 1996, INS Special Agent William West testified that al-Najjar was a "mid-level operative" in both the ICP and WISE, which he characterized as "front groups" [35] for the Palestinian Islamic Jihad in the United States. Evidence against Mazen al-Najjar included a number of documents in his possession: Islamic Jihad fax communiqués announcing the "martyrdom" of a battalion leader in 1992 and claiming credit for an attack on Israelis; detailed biographies of Hizballah, Hamas, and Islamic Jihad leaders; and an ICP draft charter containing incendiary provisions calling for the destruction of Israel and aggressive confrontation with the West.

Despite the fact that al-Najjar had been ordered deported based on visa violations and was incarcerated by the INS pursuant to, and pending the execution of, his deportation, on October 27, 2000, Immigration Judge Kevin McHugh ordered al-Najjar released on bond unless the government provided classified information to the Court that would warrant the continued detention of al-Najjar. On December 6, 2000, McHugh ordered al-Najjar released on the grounds that the government's classification of the evidence against al-Najjar had not afforded him the opportunity to defend himself against the charges and had thus violated his due process rights under the Constitution. The Eleventh Circuit Court of Appeals has since upheld the orders of deportation against both al-Najjar and his wife, and on November 24, 2001, al-Najjar was arrested yet again.

* * *

Palestinian Islamic Jihad's strong connection to the University of South Florida serves notice to law enforcement officials, universities, and the media. A major terrorist group, associating itself with a tax-exempt entity and a mainstream religious group, was able to shield itself from scrutiny for at least five years.

On September 26, 2001, shortly after the attack on the World Trade Center and the Pentagon, Sami al-Arian appeared on Fox TV's *The O'Reilly Factor,* where host Bill O'Reilly questioned him in detail about the relation between WISE and the Islamic Jihad. When al-Arian responded evasively, O'Reilly read from the transcript of several ICP rallies prior to 1995 in which al-Arian had trumpeted "Death to Israel" and its allies. Al-Arian, not surprisingly, tried to shift the subject but O'Reilly was persistent and tenacious. After this appearance, the University of South Florida was bombarded with hostile phone calls and e-mails. Al-Arian was put on indefinite paid administrative leave, his second such stint (the first coming after the FBI's 1995 search of al-Arian's home and office). More exposure came in the form of a memorable *Dateline* segment on NBC, which comprehensively explored al-Arian's activities.

As the *St. Petersburg Times* wrote in an apologetic editorial on November 1, 2001, "He [Al-Arian] has been playing his American hosts for fools for years, presenting a benign face to the general public while spewing the most hateful sort of venom in the company of fellow Islamic extremists. . . . But he'll never again get away with the pretense that his ugly support for terrorism has been misunderstood." [36]

That Sami al-Arian continues to draw his salary as a tenured professor is a tribute to the strength of academic freedoms in this country. After all, he has never been charged with any crime, much less convicted of one. With liberties like these, why wouldn't the international jihad movement want to settle here?

Chapter Seven

OSAMA BIN LADEN, SHEIKH ABDULLAH AZZAM, AND THE BIRTH OF AL QAEDA

E VERYONE KNOWS THE STORY of Osama bin Laden—how he went to Afghanistan to fight the Russians and ended up waging jihad against the entire Western world. But how many know of his predecessor Sheikh Abdullah Azzam, the Palestinian refugee who first preached worldwide jihad and laid the groundwork for bin Laden's rise to power? In fact it was Azzam's spellbinding oratory that inspired the 24-year-old Osama bin Laden to leave the comfort of his Saudi Arabian family empire in 1985 and move to Afghanistan to fight the Soviets. Moreover, Azzam's Alkhifa network—originally a fund-raiser for the Afghan mujahideen—eventually metamorphosed into bin Laden's al Qaeda ("The Base"), which is now terrorizing the world.

Most important is how both Azzam and bin Laden were able to use Islamic organizations in the United States to build their networks. It was the records of Azzam's Alkhifa organization that we spirited out of the Brooklyn basement when they had been moved there from the Al-Farook Mosque after the first World Trade Center bombing. It was in the United States that Azzam did much of his early fund-raising. It is through Islamic networks in the U.S. that bin Laden has shopped for much of the high-tech gear that runs his worldwide network. Indeed, after Hamas, al Qaeda has achieved a greater penetration on American soil than any other single group. The Investigative Project has even been on the trail of a tantalizing possibility: Osama himself may have once applied for a U.S. visa.

*   *   *

In 1993, immediately following the first World Trade Center bombing, federal prosecutors and FBI agents reexamined raw materials, documents, and data they had collected after the assassination of Rabbi Meir Kahane by El Sayeed Nosair in November 1990 and the murder (still unsolved) of the fundamentalist head of the Alkhifa office in Brooklyn, Mustapha Shalabi, in February 1991. The boxes of material seized from Nosair's apartment following his arrest in 1990 contained the very seeds of the World Trade Center explosion, but these materials also provided at least a partial road map to understanding and reconstructing the bin Laden network. In particular, new attention was focused on the Alkhifa Refugee Center, also known as the Office of Services for the

Mujahideen, that gave birth, as prosecutors laid out in their complaints and indictments, to bin Laden's secret terrorist organization. The Alkhifa Center was established in the early 1980s in Peshawar, Pakistan, by Azzam.

Born in Palestine in 1941, Abdullah Azzam moved to Jordan, then to Saudi Arabia before migrating to Pakistan at the start of the Soviet invasion of Afghanistan in 1979. Starting with not much more than a storefront in Peshawar, Azzam ultimately succeeded in reviving the concept of jihad among the Muslim masses.

People who met Azzam were always dazzled by his spellbinding oratory, his religious scholarship, his abilities as a military strategist, and his interminable energy. The bearded, barrel-chested sheikh hated the West, specifically Christians and Jews, whom he routinely accused of carrying out diabolical conspiracies against Islam. Combined with this was nostalgia for the days of the Ottoman Empire and the Islamic caliphate, when non-Muslims were the ones who were treated as second-class citizens.

It was in the United States that Azzam was able to raise much of his money, enlist new fighters, and—most important—enjoy the political freedom to coordinate with other radical Islamic movements. From 1985 to 1989, Azzam and his top aide, Palestinian Sheikh Tamim al-Adnani, visited dozens of American cities, exhorting new recruits to pick up the sword against the enemies of Islam. They raised tens of thousands of dollars and enlisted hundreds and hundreds of fighters and believers.

The First Conference of Jihad was held at the Al-Farook Mosque on Atlantic Avenue in Brooklyn in 1988. In a speech recorded on videotape, Azzam instructed his audience of nearly two hundred to carry out jihad no matter where they were, even in America. "Every Moslem on earth should unsheathe his sword and fight to liberate Palestine," he shouted in Arabic. "The jihad is not limited to Afghanistan. . . . Jihad means fighting. . . . You must fight in any place you can get . . . Whenever jihad is mentioned in the Holy Book, it means the obligation to fight. It does not mean to fight with the pen or to write books or articles in the press or to fight by holding lectures." [1]

Azzam's Office of Services started off in Peshawar, but by the end of the decade, he had succeeded in establishing scores of jihad recruiting centers around the world, in addition to a network of mosques and Islamic centers that joined the jihad orbit. Azzam had also motivated tens of thousands of Arabs from all over the world to volunteer for jihad.

By 1985, according to his own statements and accounts published by the Office of Services in its banner publication *Al-Jihad*, Azzam had teamed up with Saudi financier Osama bin Laden. Bin Laden would soon emerge as the largest single financial backer of the Office of Services for the Mujahideen and of the "Arab-Afghan" jihad movement. Having heard the call of Sheikh Azzam to join the jihad, bin Laden left the comfort of his family's multi-billion dollar construction company in Saudi Arabia to participate in the jihad against the Russians. During the 1980s, however, bin Laden scrupulously stayed behind the scenes, far away from the glare of publicity.

Azzam opened branches of the Office of Services in the United States, Britain, France, Germany, Sweden, Norway, and throughout the Middle East. Dozens of centers opened throughout the United States, mostly at mosques and Islamic community centers. Major Alkhifa Centers were set up in Atlanta, Boston, Chicago, Brooklyn, Jersey City, Pittsburgh, and Tucson, while thirty other American cities were the sites of subsidiary Alkhifa offices.

The Office of Services published a monthly magazine called *Al-Jihad*, a full-color Arabic-language magazine that detailed the battle stories from the front lines of the mujahideen. The issues were frequently full of gory pictures of young men whose limbs had been severed as well as inspiring eulogies to the *shahids* (martyrs) who gave their lives for jihad. In its heyday, *Al-Jihad* reached 50,000 people, at least half in the United States, according to interviews with *Al-Jihad* leaders. *Al-Jihad* was distributed within the United States by the Tucson, Arizona, and Brooklyn, New York, Alkhifa centers. Articles frequently contained incendiary attacks and conspiratorial allegations against the United States, Europe, Christians, and Jews, exposing their "crimes" against Islam. From Palestine to Bosnia, *Al-Jihad* called for Muslims to pick up the gun and wage jihad to kill the infidels and "all enemies of Islam."

After the Soviet Union crumbled, the duty of jihad was expanded around the globe—to any place that the enemies of Islam were deemed active. Beyond mobilizing support for the jihad in Afghanistan, internal documents show that Alkhifa members in the United States became involved in shipping bombs, timers, and explosives to Hamas in Gaza; counterfeiting tens of thousands of dollars for the purchase of weapons; reconfiguring passports to enable Muslim volunteers to visit the United States as well as to enter jihad battle fronts; and raising money and enlisting new recruits for the jihad in the Philippines, Egypt, Bosnia, Algeria, Kashmir, Palestine, and elsewhere.

Abdullah Azzam explained the new worldwide focus at gatherings of the faithful within the United States. At a conference of the Muslim Arab Youth Association (MAYA) in Oklahoma City in December 1988, Azzam inspired participants to even loftier goals: "O brothers, after our experience of Afghanistan, nothing in the world is impossible for us any more! Small power or big power, what is decisive is the willpower that springs from the religious belief." He insisted that "It has been revealed that you should perform Jihad with your lives and your wealth." [2] Azzam also made clear that Afghanistan would be used as a training ground where Muslims from around the world could receive preparation for taking the jihad to their respective regions: "The Palestinian youth came here to Afghanistan, and also non-Palestinians, and they were trained, and their souls became prepared, and the paranoia of fear disappeared, and they became experts. Now, every one of them returns . . . ready to die." [3]

*   *   *

Azzam's success in the United States is exemplified by the story of the Islamic Center of Tucson. This center during the late 1980s and early 1990s also served as the Tucson branch of Alkhifa and the Office of Services. One of Azzam's key lieutenants in Pakistan, Wa'il Jalaidan, came from the Islamic Center of Tucson in the early 1980s. Wadih el Hage, bin Laden's personal secretary in the early 1990s, was also an active member of the Islamic Center of Tucson in the mid-1980s prior to relocating to Arlington, Texas, before leaving for Sudan and Kenya to aid in bin Laden's efforts there.

Tucson, not coincidentally, has been a fertile city for terrorists. When Ramzi Yousef and Ahmed Ajaj, plotters in the first World Trade Center bombing, arrived in the U.S. in 1992, they carried identification tags listing them as working for the Al Bunyan Islamic Information Center in Tucson.

Even the Islamic Association for Palestine (IAP) used Tucson as the base for its Information Office in the late 1980s. It was from an IAP post office box address in Tucson that the organization published and disseminated, in brochure form, the "Charter of the Islamic Resistance Movement—Hamas" in 1988. Ghassan Dahduli, an IAP leader who had registered this post office box, was a member of the Board of Directors of the Islamic Center of Tucson in the mid-1980s. (Dahduli, who also moved to Arlington, Texas, in the early-1990s, has since been deported from the United States based on visa violations although authorities had collected evidence showing ties to terrorists as well.)

For Azzam, Tucson was just a starting point in the U.S., at a time when his power was growing everywhere. By the end of the 1980s, with the Soviets no longer in Afghanistan, a Muslim alliance had joined forces to rule that country, and mujahideen were branching out to other conflicts including the one most dear to Azzam, the jihad in Palestine. Meanwhile bin Laden was playing a central role in Azzam's network. In a speech given in Peshawar in 1989, Sheikh Azzam told his followers, "There is one person who has always stood by us. That is Osama bin Laden."

In November 1989, Azzam, along with two of his four sons,

was killed in a sophisticated car bombing in Pakistan. In the wake of Azzam's death, a power struggle soon developed for control of Alkhifa, not in Pakistan but in the United States, where Sheikh Omar Abdel Rahman vied with Mustapha Shalabi, an Egyptian-born militant appointed by Azzam. The sheikh settled in Brooklyn and New Jersey where he had already developed an intensely loyal following among a cadre of Islamic militants.

At stake in the battle over Alkhifa was a transnational Islamic militant power base: the de facto control over hundreds of thousands of dollars and a network of thousands of jihad veterans and future jihad volunteers. Shalabi wanted to plow the money back into the Afghanistan effort, while Sheikh Abdel Rahman wanted to expend the funds on jihad in Egypt and new jihad fronts around the globe.

Shalabi, who by all accounts resented the intrusion of the sheikh, tried to stand up to him and his supporters, especially Mahmud Abouhalima, an Egyptian veteran of the Afghanistan jihad and a loyal follower of the blind sheikh. By early January 1990, Shalabi had received threats from the sheikh's followers, but still would not agree to hand over control of the funds. Shalabi hoped to move back to Afghanistan where he could count on the protection of Mohammed Yusuf Abbas, who had taken over the Peshawar-based Office of Services and editorship of *Al-Jihad*. Shalabi would never make it. On February 26, 1991, Shalabi opened the door to someone he knew (according to police). His body was found five days later with a bullet hole to his head and multiple stab wounds. No one was ever charged in the killing, but federal officials believe that Shalabi was killed pursuant to a *fatwa* issued by Sheikh Omar Abdel Rahman.

The man who was supposed to take over the Alkhifa offices in Brooklyn as successor to Shalabi was Wadih el-Hage. Born in Lebanon in 1960, el-Hage had come to the United States in the late 1970s to attend school at the University of Southwestern Louisiana in Lafayette. In 1987, he moved to Tucson, where he became an active member of the Alkhifa office at the Islamic Center. He soon became caught up in the jihad fervor, catching the attention of senior Alkhifa officials in both Tucson and New York.

In December 1988, according to federal documents, el-Hage met other Islamic fundamentalists, including Mahmud Abouhalima and top officials of the Alkhifa Center, at a major radical Islamic conference held at the convention center in Oklahoma City. The conference was sponsored by the Muslim Arab Youth Association and the Islamic Association for Palestine. Abdullah Azzam was the keynote speaker. Videotapes of the conference and other records show that Islamic militants from around the globe converged in Oklahoma City to raise the banner of jihad not only in Afghanistan but in Palestine and elsewhere. Feverish exhortations to carry out terrorist attacks were made by Azzam and the other guest speakers, which included Hamas leader Muhammad Siyyam, militant cleric Ahmed al-Qattan, radical cleric from Lebanon Sheikh Muharram al-Aarifi, and a leader of the Muslim Brotherhood, Mustapha Mash'hur, who currently serves as the Supreme Guide of the Muslim Brotherhood in Egypt, the highest position of leadership in the organization.

Wadih el-Hage was not just watching and listening to mujahideen. In early 1990, U.S. law enforcement officials say he became involved in a murder. The victim was a black Muslim cleric named Rashid Khalifa, who was preaching a variation of Islamic doctrine that was deemed heretical by fundamentalists. According to federal prosecutors and to information volunteered by Wadih el-Hage in interviews he gave to FBI agents, a still unidentified man was sent to Tucson to conduct surveillance on Khalifa. This person visited el-Hage at his home, where they had lunch together, and then was driven by el-Hage to Khalifa's mosque, where the visitor recorded the movements of Khalifa. El-Hage admitted before a grand jury that he never reported this visit to the authorities.

Federal records show that Khalifa was killed by a member of the Al-Fuqra organization, a black Muslim fundamentalist group that has engaged in a series of murders, robberies, and other attacks in Colorado and Canada. Members of Al-Fuqra were also indicted and convicted in the World Trade Center bombing-conspiracy trials. Sources familiar with the investigation say that Al-Fuqra was as early as 1988 acquiring weapons and recruiting volunteers for the jihad in Afghanistan.

From Tucson, el-Hage moved to Arlington, Texas, sometime in 1991, where he went to work for a tire store. At the same time, according to federal prosecutors, he stayed very active with Alkhifa and on the expanding jihad battlefront. El-Hage would rise to such a senior position that he was named the successor to Alkhifa director Shalabi.

For reasons still unknown, El-Hage did not ultimately take over the Alkhifa office in Brooklyn as had been expected. According to his own statements, he showed up in New York on the day Shalabi was killed; the length of his stay is unknown. Phone records of the Alkhifa office show a series of phone calls between

Alkhifa and el-Hage's residence in Arlington, Texas on March 2, 3, 5, and 6. It appears that el-Hage was calling his home from Brooklyn. Prison records show that on March 11, 1991, el-Hage visited el-Sayeed Nosair in jail. Nosair, prosecutors later determined, had been secretly plotting to carry out additional terrorist attacks and murders while meeting with various visitors in his jail cell in 1991 and 1992.

Soon thereafter, Wadih el-Hage left the United States in order to serve as Osama bin Laden's personal secretary. In this capacity, el-Hage worked for various bin Laden companies, which included a holding company known as "Wadi al-Aqiq," a construction business known as "Al Hijra," an agricultural company known as "al Themar al Mubaraka," an investment company known as "Ladin International," another investment company known as "Taba Investments," and a transportation company known as "Qudarat Transport Company." These companies earned income to support what was now al Qaeda and provided cover for the procurement of explosives, weapons, and chemicals and for the travel of al Qaeda operatives.

Sometime in 1994, el-Hage moved from Khartoum to Nairobi where he set up businesses and other organizations for al Qaeda in Kenya. There, el-Hage met repeatedly with Abu Ubaidah al Banshiri, a former al Qaeda military commander. In 1996, however, Banshiri drowned, or was drowned. El-Hage investigated the death with Fazul Abdullah Mohammed, who later became an at-large indictee for the bombing of the U.S. embassies in Kenya and Tanzania.

Eventually, el-Hage would make false statements in September and October 1997 to both the FBI and the grand jury that was investigating Osama bin Laden regarding his role in al Qaeda. At some date prior to this, el-Hage had returned to the United States. El-Hage would be questioned again by the FBI on August 20, 1998, following the bombing of the U.S. embassies in Kenya and Tanzania on August 7. Again he would lie to the federal agents regarding his connections with al Qaeda. He then would commit perjury before the federal grand jury in New York on September 16, 1998. Wadih el-Hage would be initially indicted for this act of perjury; later the indictment would be expanded to include charges of conspiring to kill U.S. nationals, eight counts of perjury before the federal grand jury, and three counts of making false statements to federal law-enforcement officers while being questioned pursuant to a grand jury investigation.

Testimony provided in the trial of el-Hage and others for their role in the bombing of the U.S. embassies has provided a good deal of information into Osama bin Laden's rise. Bin Laden returned to Saudi Arabia for a brief interval after the Afghanistan victory of the mujahideen. By this time, the Gulf War turned him against the Saudi regime, and his criticisms caused the regime to strip him of his Saudi passport. Set loose upon the world again, bin Laden found refuge in the country that was rapidly becoming the worldwide center of international terrorism—Sudan.

A desert nation directly south of Egypt, Sudan was governed by the National Islamic Front party under Dr. Hassan al-Turabi, who seized power through a military coup in 1989. Al-Turabi did two things: he imposed a fundamentalist regime almost identical to the Ayatollah Khomeini's rule in Iran except based on Sunni principles, and he opened up Sudan to worldwide terrorists. Al-Turabi's comrade-in-arms in the coup that established the Islamic state in Sudan, Sudanese president Omar Bashir, personally welcomed al Qaeda to the country. He gave the terror organization special permission to avoid taxes and import duties and even exempted it from local law enforcement. (Sudan was not alone in sponsoring al Qaeda. Hizzbollah was happy to contribute. Hizzbollah officials arranged special advanced weapons and explosives training for mujahideen in Lebanon. Among the items on the curriculum were instructions on how to blow up large buildings.)

Soon Sudan was hosting an entire spectrum of radical Islamic groups that would plague both the Middle East and the West and foster political unrest around the world. As low-cost, low-tech weapons became more accessible, Sudan-based terrorists found it easier to export death and destruction worldwide, including to the most technically advanced nations.

To pick a random list, Sudan-based terrorists instigated:

- Suicide bombings in Israel
- The attempted assassination of the president of Egypt
- A brutal military campaign of near-genocidal proportions against the black non-Muslim tribal minorities in southern Sudan
- Attacks on American forces in Somalia
- Unparalleled get-togethers of the world's most militant Islamic terrorist leaders

- Training camps for weapons and explosives

- Training camps for Iranian Revolutionary Guards—who in turn trained street militias called the Popular Defense Forces, who carry out vigilante violence

- Use of the Sudanese diplomatic pouch to transport explosives

- Support of terrorist attacks in Ethiopia

- Support for, advance knowledge of, and critical involvement with the second series of planned terrorist attacks in Manhattan following the original World Trade Center bombing

Although Iran sponsored more terrorism than Sudan during this period, Dr. al-Turabi's regime was more focused than any other on supporting the global Muslim Brotherhood. His Popular Arab Islamic Conferences—three in all—were unprecedented gatherings that featured a global panorama of the Islamic movement, including delegations from the Middle East, Spain, France, Italy, Argentina, Mexico, Canada, Kenya, and the United States.

There were plenty of critics of Sudan in the international community. In response, apologists for Dr. al-Turabi liked to claim that Sudan was singled out only because of its Islamic identity. In August 1994, for example, *The Atlantic Monthly* published "Turabi's Law," an article by William Langewiesche that exposed in chilling detail the totalitarian religious code that was being imposed by the Sudanese government. In a letter to the editor two months later, Ibrahim Hooper, director of communications of the

Council on American-Islamic Relations (CAIR), attacked the article for making "many negative assertions about Islam, Shariah, Sudan and Hassan al-Turabi." Hooper denied the existence of Sudanese secret police and criticized the article for "merely rehashed Western clichés about 'fundamentalism' and Islamic radicalism [while] ignor[ing] non-Islamic causes of Sudan's turmoil."[4]

There were non-Muslim apologists as well. In 1993, when Sudan was placed on the State Department's list of countries supporting terrorism, Jimmy Carter expressed his disdain for the decision. "They declared that Sudan was a terrorist training center, I think without proof," said the former president. "In fact, when I later asked an assistant secretary of state he said they did not have proof, but there were strong allegations. . . . I think there is too much of an inclination in this country to look at Muslims as inherently terrorist or inherently against the West. . . . I don't see that when I meet with these people."[5]

The urbane, British-and-French-educated Hassan al-Turabi, with a doctorate from the Sorbonne, obviously made a strong impression on the former president. Yet if it is wrong to consider all Muslims terrorists, so is it wrong to assume that all Muslim militants carry automatic weapons, wear scruffy beards, and shout "Death to America." Many are highly sophisticated Westernized intellectuals. Daniel Pipes, director of the Middle East Forum, has argued that it is precisely the Westernized intellectuals in Muslim countries who are most susceptible to anti-Americanism and Islamic militancy. The posture seems to represent, in part, a recoil from the stresses of trying to assimilate to another culture.

As a semi-Westernized intellectual, Dr. al-Turabi is skillful in telling other Westerners what they want to hear. Speaking in the London-based *Al-Quds al-Arabi,* Dr. al-Turabi defended Islam by arguing, "We have a heritage and a wealth of culture but their [the West's] life has been culturally empty. Even their music is now more like loud noise than serious music. They no longer know or read books. They are content with just watching television and switching from one channel to another." [6] Many Westerners would obviously agree—although they wouldn't necessarily resort to terrorism as a consequence. At other times, Dr. al-Turabi has been more blunt: "The enemy is America," he told *The London Daily Telegraph* on August 15, 1995. "If we are challenged economically we will develop our own country, we are very rich; if we are challenged culturally we will develop our own culture; if we are challenged militarily, we will have to fight back."

It was not long before Sudan was doing just that. Evidence produced at the trial of the Day of Terror bombings, plus information obtained by federal law-enforcement agents, shows that top officials of the Sudanese regime not only knew in advance of the foiled "Day of Terror" but actively facilitated the plot. Taped conversations linked the defendants with members of the Sudanese government. In those tapes, Siddiq Ali, a translator for the blind sheikh and the Sudanese ringleader of the Day of Terror, openly proclaimed that "our relation is very, very, very, very strong with the Sudanese government, and with the Islamic leaderships of Sudan, thanks to God that I have a direct contact with the Islamic leaders themselves." [7] In the same conversation, Ali stated that his ties were so close to Sudanese officials in the United States that he could walk right into the office of the Sudanese ambassador to the United Nations, the Sudanese consul, and the vice consul.

"When we hit the United Nations, it will teach the world, the world, not only America a lesson," Siddiq Ali declared in discussing the plan to blow up U.N. headquarters. Ali told fellow conspirators he could obtain critical help from Sudanese U.N. diplomats in securing credentials, license plates, and ID cards. This would enable them to drive an explosives-laden Lincoln Town Car right into the parking garage adjacent to U.N. headquarters. Sudanese officials were aware of the plan, Ali stated.

When Siddiq Ali began to conspire to assassinate Egyptian president Hosni Mubarak, who was scheduled to visit New York City that spring, the Sudanese mission in New York provided him with acutely sensitive information about how to pierce President Mubarak's security detail as it drove him from Kennedy Airport to his suite at the Waldorf Astoria. In a chilling conversation taped by Emad Salem, Ali told his coconspirators the exact route of Mubarak's U.S. Secret Service detail, even specifying the precise car in the police motorcade in which the president would be riding. Asked by Emad Salem where he got this information, Ali responded, " I get it from the highest level . . . from people inside the [Sudanese] Embassy. . . . My contact is the ambassador, brother."

Siddiq Ali was not the only Sudanese connection to the terrorist plot. Another defendant was Mohammed Saleh, a Yonkers gasoline-station operator who was to provide the fuel for the explosive device. According to information obtained by federal investigators, Saleh was a Hamas operative in charge of training terrorist recruits in Sudan. He had also bought terrorist tools, including guns and night-vision goggles, which were ultimately smuggled to Hamas squads in the West Bank. Mr. Saleh's home in the Bronx was a safe house for terrorists visiting the United States, including Jordanian militant and recruiter of Hamas terrorists, Ahmed Noufal.

Eventually, relations between the United States and Sudan chilled. Two Sudanese diplomats in New York were expelled in 1986; nevertheless, in early 1997, a Sudanese intelligence officer who once worked in Washington, D.C., sought entry to the United States under false documentation. His mission was to expand the Sudanese terrorist network on behalf of the National Islamic Front. Working secretly at night out of the Washington offices of the America Muslim Council for almost a year, this operative was able to establish close ties between Islamic groups in the United States and members of the Muslim Brotherhood in the Middle East. This information was revealed to me by a former AMC official, who was genuinely repelled by the fact that an American Muslim group would work hand-in-hand with such a brutal regime.

By far the most damaging result of Sudan's sponsorship of terrorism was the rise of Osama bin Laden, who came into his own during the years he spent there. Bin Laden sponsored the arrival of nearly 2,000 mujahideen from Afghanistan, who lived under his care. Bin Laden also became extremely active in terrorist activities around the world. In the late 1990s trial of the African embassy bombings, former bin Laden lieutenant Jamal Ahmed al-Fadl, a Sudanese who absconded with some of bin Laden's money in 1994, said that he personally smuggled four crates of explosives from bin Laden's farm at Soba to rebels in Yemen. Al-Fadl also claimed to have led a camel caravan loaded with Kalashnikovs to Egypt. Utilizing both his money and his construction expertise, bin Laden helped Sudan's ruling NIF build what was at that point the world's largest complex of terrorist training camps. Among the sites were:

- The al-Khalafiyya area, roughly twenty-five miles north of Khartoum, where Algerian Islamic Salvation Army and Armed Islamic Group members trained

- The Akhil al-Awliya, on the banks of the Blue Nile south of Khartoum, where at any one time upwards of five hundred Palestinians, Syrians, and Jordanians actively trained

- Al Mrihat, north of Umm Durman, where Egyptian members of the Muslim Brotherhood, the Jama'at Islamiyya, and the Vanguards trained

- Mukhayyamat al-Mazari, northwest of Khartoum, which served as an equal-opportunity training center for all nationalities, including Libyans, Tunisians, Palestinians, Syrians, Saudis, Lebanese, and Algerians. Even several Americans were known to have passed through.

Bin Laden's years in Sudan overlapped with many other terrorists' residencies, and helped him turn al Qaeda into a global umbrella organization. Among his Sudanese compatriots were the conspirators who failed in a brazen attempt to assassinate Egyptian president Hosni Mubarak on June 26, 1995, in Addis Ababa. These well-equipped killers—who possessed rocket grenade launchers, anti-tank missiles, explosives, and automatic weapons—failed only because of the tardiness of Mubarak's motorcade. Credit was claimed by al-Gama'at al-Islamiyya, whose members were trained in the Sudan. Dr. al-Turabi personally blocked their subsequent extradition. In September 1995, the Organization of African Unity condemned Sudan for supporting the attack and called upon the regime to turn over three suspects. Ethiopian Foreign Minister Seyoum Mesfin also charged that Sudan was using diplomatic cover to smuggle weapons and explosives into Ethiopia.

Al-Gama'at al-Islamiyya was hardly the only group there, however. The Palestinian Islamic Jihad, a militant cadre that specializes in dismembering and mutilating its victims, used Sudan as a base. Dr. al-Turabi gave diplomatic passports to Palestinian Islamic Jihad leaders such as Sheikh Abdel Aziz Odeh and Fathi Shikaki, who was killed in Malta in October 1995—to be replaced by Ramadan Abdullah Shallah of the University of South Florida. Employing Iranian funds, al-Turabi was able to help the Palestinian Islamic Jihad to return to Israel, where it carried out extensive terror operations. Hamas, Algerian Islamic Salvation Army fighters, Iranian Revolutionary Guards, and al-Gama'at al-Islamiyya also relied on Sudan. By 1995, half the 3,000 Iranian Revolutionary Guards sent to Khartoum had come from Lebanon. Of these, more that 1,000 were Lebanese Hizballah.

Until he arrived in Sudan, Osama bin Laden's greatest accomplishment had been his financial backing of Ramzi Yousef, mastermind of the World Trade Center bombing, who was now formulating plots to bomb a series of American aircraft flying from the Far East. In Sudan, bin Laden began assembling a worldwide network of front companies, Islamic charities, nongovernmental organizations, and recruitment centers that would help carry out attacks against American, Egyptian, Israeli, Saudi, and European targets. In the process, bin Laden helped the Sudanese build an airport in Port Sudan, an ocean port, and a network of north-to-south roads. In return, the NIF gave their guest monopolistic control over Sudanese agricultural exports and exclusive purchase rights over large domains of farmland.

In the early 1990s, bin Laden sponsored his first effort against the United States—Muslim militias that attacked the U.S. servicemen sent to Somalia to protect civilians. The result was a stunning defeat for the United States, which included the gruesome spectacle of dead American soldiers being dragged through the streets of Mogadishu. The encounter emboldened bin Laden, who said later he was surprised how quickly the American government was willing to retreat.

Next, U.S. authorities believe—but do not have "smoking gun" evidence—that the Saudi expatriate directed twin attacks against barracks housing U.S. servicemen on the Arabian peninsula in November 1995 and June 1996. More than a dozen American were killed and scores more wounded. In May 1996, Dr. al-Turabi finally yielded to diplomatic pressure from the United States and other countries and deported bin Laden. The wealthy Saudi refugee was offered the chance to renounce his jihad and return to Saudi Arabia. Instead, he went back to Afghanistan, where the Taliban had now overrun much of the northern region of the country. There, bin Laden began plotting terrorist acts that would one day announce his declaration of war to every American.

In the fall of 1996, Osama bin Laden issued a 60-page *fatwa,* soon dubbed the "Ladenese Epistle." It constituted a formal declaration of war against the United States. "Clearly, after Belief, there is no more important duty than pushing the American enemy out of the Holy Land," bin Laden wrote. "Due to the imbalance of power between our armed forces and the enemy forces, a suitable means of fighting must be adopted, i.e., using fast-moving light forces that work under complete secrecy. In other words to initiate a guerrilla warfare, where the sons of the nation, and not the military forces, take part in it."[8]

The Epistle is a remarkable document. It revealed a hitherto unexpressed articulateness in bin Laden. In fact, it was so brilliant that bin Laden was forced to defend himself from public charges in the Islamic community that he had used a ghost-writer. Predictably, the Epistle dripped with rage against "crusaders" (the Christian West) and Jews, invoking incendiary citations from Islamic militant theology that mandated a war to avenge the "attack on Islam." Obviously approaching paranoia, bin Laden raged against the United States for nearly every adverse event ever suffered by the Muslim *Ummah* (nation)—even though the *Ummah* predates the founding of the United States by nearly a millennium.

Bin Laden's 1996 declaration of war was virtually ignored by the American media, an omission not unnoticed by bin Laden himself. To correct this oversight, he began giving interviews to Arab and Western journalists from his hideout in Afghanistan. In each interview he was careful to repeat his avowed threats to attack the United States. Then, on February 23, 1998, he issued a new *fatwa* calling for Muslims to kill Americans and Jews everywhere in the world. This time his declarations were noticed by the CIA, which sent a memorandum to Congress warning that bin Laden was authorizing terrorist attacks on Americans throughout the world. Inside the government, there was growing awareness that bin Laden was a very dangerous person, ready to unleash death and destruction wherever he could. The only question was when and where.

Most of what was known about Osama bin Laden at that point appeared in the investigations of a New York grand jury. In 1996, when bin Laden operatives Ramzi Yousef and Wali Khan Amin Shah were convicted in the trial of the first World Trade Center bombing and a plot to bomb American airliners in the Philippines, Shah soon began cooperating with the grand jury investigating the "Day of Terror" case. Other bin Laden followers had defected after arrests in Saudi Arabia and Egypt, but this was the first significant breakthrough.

Through foreign intelligence channels, timely analysis of electronic intelligence overseas, and the information gleaned from Shah and other informants, federal officials' worst fears were confirmed: Osama bin Laden intended to strike at the United States in a series of bomb attacks, although the identity of the targets could not be determined. Unfortunately, the evidence tying bin Laden to other terrorist schemes was circumstantial. His connections to the bombing of American servicemen in Saudi Arabia in 1995 and 1996 were even weaker. The 1997 arrest in Saudi Arabia of Hani al-Sayegh, suspected of participating in the 1996 attack on U.S. troops in that country, provided prosecutors with one link. But the case quickly fell apart when al-Sayegh recanted his confession and withdrew his guilty plea. It was in June of 1997, as a result of mounting evidence of the strength of al Qaeda and other groups, that I stated in an interview that America should "get ready for twenty World Trade Center bombings."[9]

By the spring of 1998, federal officials finally felt confident in pursuing an indictment against him. But this left one huge question—how could bin Laden be arrested? The decision about whether to use American forces in a raid to arrest bin Laden could only be decided at the presidential level. Within the government, some argued that spilling American blood to arrest bin Laden would be a Pyrrhic victory—particularly if he were subsequently acquitted in the legal process. The case against him certainly wasn't foolproof. Still, many argued that a commando-style arrest should be pursued.

Then on the morning of August 7, 1998, the U.S. embassies in Kenya and Tanzania were bombed nine minutes apart by members of al Qaeda, who drove trucks filled with explosives into them. It was hardly the most successful operation of Osama bin Laden's organization. No Americans died in the Tanzania bombing, but eleven Tanzanians did. In Nairobi, 201 Kenyans and twelve Americans were killed in the explosion.

Outraged, President Clinton lobbed a few cruise missiles into Afghanistan, trying to hit bin Laden's underground headquarters. He also pursued two more tracks: preparing a commando arrest team for insertion into Afghanistan, while at the same time getting the Taliban to cooperate in forcing the surrender of bin Laden to the United States. U.S. Ambassador to the United Nations Bill Richardson was dispatched to Afghanistan and Pakistan to negotiate with the Taliban for the handover of bin

Laden. Yet after months of discussions at various levels of both governments, nothing happened.

The U.S. military effort finally petered out. President Clinton and the rest of the country were distracted by the Monica Lewinsky scandal. Events in Afghanistan seemed very remote. An entire Presidential election and change of administration occurred without any further developments. On the legal front, however, major progress was made. Four men were quickly arrested after the bombing and in 2001, a New York federal jury returned guilty verdicts against all four, including Wadih el-Hage. The exhibits and trial proceedings provided a riveting view into the shadowy world of al Qaeda. The evidence revealed an umbrella organization that shelters a wide range of Islamist groups, including Hizballah, Islamic Jihad, and the Armed Islamic Group, plus a raft of Iraqi, Sudanese, Pakistani, Afghan, and Jordanian terror "cells." Each functions semi-autonomously and has the capacity to carry out its own recruiting and operations. All these groups coordinate through al Qaeda's "Shura Council," a kind of board of directors that includes representatives from all the constituents far and wide. The board meets on a regular basis in Afghanistan to review and approve proposed operations. Most representatives have maintained close relationships with each other since the end of the war in Afghanistan against the Soviets. They are a smooth and efficient operation.

We learned from the trial that when operations in one place are shut down, the rest of the network soldiers on, virtually unaffected. Even if bin Laden himself were to be killed, this Islamist network would survive and in all likelihood continue to expand, sustained by its ideological adhesion. Islamism is the fuel that fires the group and the glue that holds it together.

Perhaps the most disconcerting revelations from the trial concern al Qaeda's entrenchment in the West. All of the organization's procurement of such materiel as night-vision goggles, construction equipment, cell phones, and satellite telephones, for example, was from the West, including from such countries as the United States, Britain, France, Germany, Denmark, Bosnia, and Croatia. Chemicals purchased for the manufacture of chemical weapons came from the Czech Republic.

During the long waits between terrorist attacks, al Qaeda's member organizations maintained readiness by operating under the cover of nonprofit, tax-deductible religious charities and civil-rights organizations. These "NGOs"—non-governmental organizations—many of which still operate, are headquartered in the United States and Britain, as well as in the Middle East. The Qatar Charitable Society, for example, was identified by a witness at the Embassy bombings trial as one of bin Laden's de facto banks, raising money and transferring funds all around the globe.

Operating in the freewheeling and tolerant environment of the United States, bin Laden was able to set up a whole array of "cells" in a loosely organized network that included Tucson, Arizona; Brooklyn, New York; Orlando, Florida; Dallas, Texas; Santa Clara, California; Columbia, Missouri; and Herndon, Virginia.

*   *   *

One of Osama bin Laden's most important "policy objectives" in his worldwide jihad has been to recruit American citizens to aid in his terrorist endeavors. Despite the loathing of the United States apparent in his accumulated statements and *fatwas,* he has understood the freedom that an American passport can confer upon its possessor. With an American passport, a bin Laden operative could travel virtually anywhere in the world without question or detection as a member of a terrorist apparatus. The indictment filed against bin Laden and his compatriots following the bombing of the U.S. embassies in Kenya and Tanzania notes that bin Laden "made efforts to recruit United States citizens . . . in order to utilize the American citizens for travel throughout the Western world to deliver messages and engage in financial transactions for the benefit of al Qaeda and its affiliated groups and to help carry out operations." [10]

I have already discussed the case of Ali Mohammed, bin Laden's "Special Operations Man" (in Chapter 3) and that of Wadih el-Hage, bin Laden's personal secretary. Another telling example of bin Laden's recruitment of American citizens is the story of Khalil Said Khalil Deek.

Deek was born in 1958 in the village of Nazlit Issa on the West Bank, which was at the time a part of the Kingdom of Transjordan. He first came to the United States to pursue university studies in computer science in 1981. In 1991, Deek became a naturalized citizen living in the suburbs of Los Angeles, California. In either 1997 or 1998, Deek moved to Peshawar, Pakistan. In the second week of December 1999, he was arrested in Pakistan and subsequently extradited to Jordan on December 17, 1999, in order to stand trial for participating in a conspiracy to carry out terrorist attacks in Jordan and for the possession and manufacturing of explosives to use unlawfully in cooperation with a number of other suspected terrorists who were arrested in Jordan. In an odd twist Deek, after being in prison in Jordan for seventeen months, was released without charge on May 23, 2001. His whereabouts are currently unknown.

The other suspected terrorists who were arrested in Jordan were convicted of plotting to carry out terrorist attacks during the millennium celebrations. Some of these individuals were even sentenced to death. At the same time, in the United States, Ahmed Ressam, an Algerian who received training in camps operated by bin Laden, was arrested when he tried to smuggle explosives, and materials used to construct explosives, over the Canadian border into Washington state. Ressam was intercepted by U.S. Customs officers at the border. After his conviction, Ressam confessed to U.S. authorities of a plot to bomb Los Angeles International Airport during the millennium celebrations.

One of Ressam's accomplices was an individual named Abu Doha. In a sealed complaint filed against Abu Doha in the Southern District of New York, it was alleged that he had conspired "to use a weapon of mass destruction . . . against persons within the United States. . . . "[11] Ressam, in compliance with a cooperation agreement with the government, stated that while training in Afghanistan, an Algerian cell was formed and that he was one of its leaders.[12] Abu Doha was to facilitate the travel of members of the cell in and out of Afghanistan and into the countries where terrorist activities were to take place.[13] Deek was doing something similar, according to the complaint: "by Deek's own account . . . Deek has helped facilitate the travel of various individuals to training camps in Afghanistan so that they may participate in Islamic jihad terrorist activities."[14] The complaint elaborated:

Recovered from Deek at the time of his arrest were various papers, computers and computer disks. Contained within this material were various terrorist training manuals as well as sketches and formulas for various explosive devices and materials. The computers were downloaded and several e-mails were retrieved. At least two of the e-mails, dated September 25 and 29, 1999, discuss providing funds, personnel, and material support for the Afghan training camps.[15]

In fact, one of the documents found in Deek's possession at his arrest was a CD-ROM version of the 7,000-page *Encyclopedia of Jihad* which provided unparalleled detail of how to conduct terrorist activities of every type. Deek was actually aiding terrorists in Afghanistan in gaining access to the training camps there, and also to different countries throughout the world. The question arises: what was he doing in the United States prior to his departure to Pakistan, and why did the Jordanian authorities release him?

As one of the first people to investigate Deek, I was able to determine that he had changed his name in 1996 to Joseph Adams. According to Deek's brother, Tawfiq Deek, who lives in Anaheim, California, this change was to facilitate Khalil's procuring a new passport in order to be able to travel to Jordan where he would be able to enter the West Bank to visit his father.[16] Deek's brother insisted that he had last been in the United States in 1997; however, information surfaced that Khalil Deek was a "crew leader" for an organization called Charity Without Borders from March through August 1998 on a contract procured from the State of California. One of the purposes of this entity, according to their own documentation, was to "educate, feed, clothe, and shelter anyone in any country that is in need of our help." In addition, Charity Without Borders received grant money from the State of California for waste disposal. Joseph Adams's name was listed on invoices submitted to the state long after he had allegedly left the United States.

Authorities suspect that some of the monies flowing through this entity might have made their way to bin Laden's organization. Deek shared a bank account with Abu Zubaydah, an alleged close associate of bin Laden. Was money from the Charity Without Borders projects with the State of California used to fund terrorist activities? We may never know the answer to this question.

*   *   *

There is a tantalizing postscript to the story of Osama bin Laden's American operations. Did Osama himself once consider coming here? We are certain that bin Laden's second-in-command of al Qaeda, Ayman al-Zawahiri of the Egyptian Al-Jihad organization, came to the United States in 1995 on a fund-raising mission. As stated by Ali Mohammed, "In the early 1990s, al-Zawahiri made two visits to the United States, and he came to United States [sic] to help raise funds for the Egyptian Islamic Jihad."[17]

If bin Laden himself considered coming to the United States, it was in connection with Mohammad Jamal Khalifa, a Jordanian resident who is bin Laden's brother-in-law. In April 1994, Khalifa was implicated by Jordanian authorities in the bombing of a theater on the outskirts of Amman. Accusing Khalifa of financing the operation, a Jordanian court put out a warrant for him. On December 1, 1994, Khalifa entered the United States after successfully applying for a visa. Even though he was under sentence of death in Jordan, he had no trouble slipping through U.S. immigration. It was not until two weeks later that U.S. officials realized their mistake. Khalifa was arrested on December 16 in Morgan Hill, California, and held without bond during deportation hearings. He was eventually extradited to Jordan and forced to stand trial with ten other defendants. While the other ten defendants were convicted and sentenced to death, Khalifa won acquittal.

During his years in the Philippines, Khalifa helped spread terror around the world while serving as president of a branch office in the Philippines of the International Islamic Relief Organization (IIRO), a charity organization funded by both private Saudi individuals and the Saudi government. Based in Jidda, Saudi Arabia, IIRO, along with its bona fide charitable efforts, provided cover for Osama bin Laden's efforts around the globe. Through IIRO, bin Laden and Khalifa supported the Abu Sayyaf Group, an Islamic terrorist group in the Philippines.[18] After the dual bombings of the U.S. embassies in Kenya and Tanzania in 1998, the government of Kenya deregistered the IIRO chapter in Nairobi for its alleged connections to the attacks. In January 1999, Indian authorities accused Sheikh al-Gamdin, president of the IIRO offices in Asia, of masterminding a plot to blow up the American consulates in Calcutta and Madras.[19] Meanwhile, according to Western intelligence experts, IIRO funneled more than $20 million a year to Islamic extremists in the West Bank and the Gaza Strip.[20] Throughout this reign of international terror, Khalifa managed to stay out of reach of the law.

The intriguing footnote is this. When Khalifa applied for an American visa in 1993, someone else applied with him. We have obtained the visa application from the state department through the Freedom of Information Act. The name is blacked out—but the individual is described as a male Saudi passport holder whose origins were in Yemen. Bin Laden's families are Yemeni nationals who live in Saudi Arabia only because of the success of his father's construction company in working with the Saudi government. Is it conceivable that in 1994 he was feeling the heat in Sudan and, like to many other international terrorists, decided to explore the possibilities of seeking temporary sanctuary in the United States? Whoever it was ultimately changed his mind and did not obtain a visa. But even the possibility is tantalizing, and chilling.

Chapter Eight

FIGHTING BACK

A Story of Unsung Heroes

D ESPITE THE FACT that militant Islamicist voices are heard from a large number of American mosques, and despite the sinister public-relations campaign of radical charitable organizations such as the American Muslim Council, the fact remains that militant Islamist views are confined to a relatively small slice of all American Muslims. Many courageous moderate Muslims have stood up to be counted against the voices of extremism—despite threats of violence. These activists are heroes, since there is no more dangerous thing to do than to denounce the faith of a fundamentalist. They deserve to be celebrated and supported in any way possible.

On January 7, 1999, one of the single most courageous of these heroes, Sheikh Muhammad Hisham Kabbani, appeared before an open forum at the U.S. State Department entitled "Islamic Extremism: A Viable Threat to U.S. National Security." A panel of State Department officials were present, along with a huge contingent of so-called leaders from the American Muslim community.

Sheikh Kabbani's testimony was a breath of fresh air. Although he represents a large organization (he is the head of the Islamic Supreme Council of America), he did not pretend to speak for all Muslims. "I cannot speak on behalf of all Muslims, as many nonprofit organizations in America do," he said. "Immediately when something happens in the Middle East, they send media alerts saying they are speaking on behalf of the whole Muslim community, which is completely incorrect. I will say that it is an opportunity to address you and to give you the authentic, traditional voice of Islam. It is a voice . . . which [stands for] moderation and tolerance and love . . . and living in peace with all other faiths and religions."

Sheikh Kabbani's most controversial assertions of the day were twofold: 80 percent of all mosques and Muslim charitable organizations in the United States had been taken over by "extremists" who did not represent the mainstream community; and Osama bin Laden represented an imminent threat to America, possibly through his attempted acquisition of nuclear weapons. In the audience were other Muslim leaders whom he was branding as extremists, and the meeting ended amid shouted accusations. Afterward, radicalized Muslim organizations immediately charged that he was slandering all Muslims. A consortium of nine Muslim organizations combined to issue a press release condemning his testimony. There were threats on his life. But in the end his warnings proved to be spectacularly prescient. Only after September 11, 2001, did members of the press belatedly realize that there was substance to what Sheikh Kabbani had been saying.

Kabbani was raised in Lebanon, the nephew of that country's grand mufti, or religious head. As a boy he traveled widely with a Sufi master (he later married his mentor's daughter). He went to high school at a French school, and then switched to an evangelical Christian academy, both in Beirut. He graduated with a chemistry degree from the American University there. With Lebanon embroiled in civil war, Kabbani came to the United States in 1991 to enlighten people about the teachings of Sufism. His Islamic Supreme Council of the Americas claims eight thousand contributors and participants, and runs 23 centers. He speaks Arabic, French, and English energetically, gesticulating and pouring words from his flowing white beard. In 1999, in a profile in the *Los Angeles Times,* he told reporter Teresa Watanabe that he planned to form a Muslim antiterrorist council to uncover the links between Muslim organizations in America and international terrorist networks. "We are afraid this [militant Islam] will spread to the United States. We are afraid this kind of doctrine controlling mosques will lead to military actions," he said.[1]

As a scholar and student of Muslim history, Sheikh Kabbani frequently enlists the story of Muhammad against modern extremists:

[Muhammad] established his first state after having received the message for thirteen years. He established a state in a city called Medina, located in Saudi Arabia now. First it had Jews, it had Christians, it had people of all kinds of different faiths, and he never fought with anyone. He never killed anyone, but was always educating and giving the message of God, as Moses, as Jesus [did]. For eighteen months [Muhammad] directed his faith to worship God toward the place of Jesus and the place of Moses, where they were born and where they brought their message, in order to show that there is a completion, and a connection between Judaism, Christianity and Islam. This was also to earn the respect of the Jews and the Christians in order to educate them about the message of Islam and show them that it is not hostile to Judaism and Christianity. It was one of the main themes in Islamic history that the Prophet tried many times to make peace treaties and to extend his hand to the Jews and to the Christians in his area, wherever he was living. Later, when the religion was well established, he turned his face towards Mecca while Jews and Christians were living in the same town.[2]

Kabbani is highly critical of the Wahhabism movement that has given birth to many of today's extremists. "It began in the seventeenth and eighteenth century," he testified.

The man who brought it to the tribes was a Muslim scholar by the name of Muhammad ibn Abd al-Wahhab. This was in the Eastern part of what we call

Saudi Arabia during the seventeenth and eighteenth century. These ideas were going forth and back. Sometimes they were put down and other times they were supported. There was a struggle with the Muslims trying to keep them down with the support of the Ottoman Empire. They were successful until the Ottoman Empire dissolved and finished in the middle of 1920 and the new regime came—it was the secular regime of Mustafa Kemal [Ataturk]. They then found an opportunity in the tribes, which no longer had the support of the Ottoman Empire in that area. They had freedom to go and change the ideas and brainwash the minds of Muslims in this area. Slowly, slowly in the many years from 1920 until today they were very successful in establishing a new ideology in Islam that is very extremist in its point of view. It was not so militant [at first], however; it didn't take the form of militancy, but it took the form of revival or renewal of Islamic tradition.[3]

Wahhabism was the religion of the al-Saud family when they unified the tribes of the Arabian Peninsula in the 1930s and seized power, establishing the Kingdom of Saudi Arabia. The Wahhabis were fierce puritans and iconoclasts, their origins beginning in the 1700s in the Arabian peninsula. They destroyed many Muslim shrines, including the graves of many of the Prophet's first followers and the Garden of Khadijah, his first wife. Visitation to tombs, they claimed, was idol-worship, a corruption of "true Islam," a view with no basis in Islamic law or doctrine.

Modern adherents of Wahhabism are tethered to Islamic militancy. "Their way of thinking is that Islam has to be reformed, and with a sword," said Sheikh Kabbani. "They think they cannot reform Islam except with the mentality of a sword and the mentality of a gun. Unfortunately, extremism appeared in Islam, but not because of Islam. Islam always presented—and I say it many times that Prophet Muhammad used to act this way with his neighbors or his friends that [were] not Muslims—[giving them] gifts, flowers, and love, not ever holding a sword against them, or ever starting a struggle or a fight against them. There are many events in Muslim history where the Prophet made peace treaties with non-Muslims."[4]

Kabbani's chief message, when he testified to the State Department, was to beware. "These people nowadays are developing two ways of understanding the situation of Islam. From one side they think that they have to reform it; it is a duty on them, they have been brainwashed to think that they have to cleanse the world of devils and demons and of countries that suppress them, oppress them, and try to shut them down. . . . I am speaking openly to give advice to the government and the U.S. officials in order to open their minds because this is a big danger that may result in a struggle within the United States."[5]

Sheikh Kabbani has, not surprisingly, angered the American Muslim establishment by charging that they have backed terror causes. For understandable reasons of self-interest, it was not a message that the American Muslim establishment wanted the American public to hear. "There have been many nonprofit organizations established in the United States whose job is only to collect money and to send it . . . to extremists outside the United

States. . . . They send it under humanitarian aid, but it doesn't go to humanitarian aid. . . . Yes, some of it will go to homeless people and poor people but the majority, 90 percent of it, will go into the black markets in these countries and [to] buying weapon arsenals."[6] He also argued that certain Muslim organizations had "hijacked the mike" in claiming to speak for the entire community.

Sheikh Kabbani is a traditional Muslim who practices the discipline of Sufism. Sufism originated in the teachings of Mohammad and was formalized into forty different schools. They seek to uphold the tenets of perfection of character and purification, parallel with the requirements of practical law and doctrine. Sufism is a much more relaxed and tolerant version of Islam, popular in the Eastern Mediterranean. The "whirling dervishes" of Turkey are Sufi Muslims. Sufis are not very popular with Muslim fundamentalists, who see them as just the sort of frivolous offshoot that they are trying to abolish in returning to the True Islam. It is not surprising to find Kabbani and the fundamentalists in disagreement.

But the important thing is this. There are many, many sides to the Islamic religion, and the existence of a strong element of militant fundamentalists is a threat not only to American institutions and lives, but also to moderate Muslims. Tarek Fatah, who hosts "The Muslim Chronicles" on Canadian television, told *The Toronto Star* he has kept his bags packed since criticizing Muslim extremism on television. "I've been getting death threats, and moderate leaders in the U.S. have also faced fierce criticism for opposing extremist regimes and North American organizations that condone the actions carried out by extremists in the name of Islam," he said. "The moderate voice is almost nonexistent."

"It saddens me that CAIR Canada has become one of the leading organizations speaking on behalf of Muslims," he added, speaking of the Canadian branch of the Council for American Islamic Relations. "And they won't even come out and formally denounce the people we know are behind the terrorism, because they have indirect support from the same groups. This nonsense of condemning the act and then wriggling out of their responsibility needs to be confronted."[7]

Some of the struggles between the fundamentalists and moderates have been well publicized. In Egypt, the Muslim Brotherhood made an unsuccessful knife attack on seventy-two-year-old Naguib Mahfouz, winner of the Nobel Prize for Literature. He was deemed "too moderate" in his religious beliefs. But such a visible hero is echoed many times over by less famous victims.

Another American unsung hero was Seifeldin ("Seif") Ashmawy, an Egyptian-born Muslim and peace activist who immigrated to the United States in search of freedom in 1969. He organized a group of like-minded moderate Muslims to form the Peace Press Association, publishing a monthly newsletter entitled *Voice of Peace*. He also appeared monthly on "Religion on the Line," a WABC-radio program, and served on the Advisory Board of the Tanenbaum Center for Interreligious Understanding. Prior to the first World Trade Center bombing, he debated Sheikh Omar Abdel Rahman in New Jersey, which shows no small amount of bravery.

Ashmawy's magazine, *Voice of Peace,* was a voice of reason. He continually exposed the pretensions of Muslim groups and pointed the way toward a more rational assessment of the religion. In 1996, he testified alongside me before the Senate Foreign Relations Committee that "most of our [Islamic] institutions in the United States are controlled by either extremists or profiteers. Both are abusing the freedom which we enjoy and . . . are being supported and financed by . . . the Saudis, Kuwaitis, and the Gulf States." [8]

Ashmawy was particularly critical of American Muslim organizations that purported to speak for all Muslims and yet, in certain cases, were radicalized and actively involved with terrorist organizations. In Senate testimony, for example, he argued that "The American Muslim Council is an umbrella group of the 'Muslim Brotherhood' and it is actively involved in championing the movements of Hamas, Algerian FIS, Tunisian Al-Nahda movement, Turkish Welfare Party, Jordanian Islamic Action Front and the Sudanese National Islamic Front. The American Muslim Council does not represent American Muslims, it represents the extremists and those that believe in terrorism." [9]

In an often-quoted letter headed "Deception in the Media," published on the MSANEWS Web site (run by the Muslim Students Association) and dated January 17, 1996, Ashmawy took both the Council on American-Islamic Relations and the American Muslim Council to task for defending Islamic extremism. "It is a known fact that both the AMC . . . and CAIR have defended, apologized for and rationalized the actions of extremist groups and leaders such as convicted World Trade Center conspirator Sheikh Omar Abdel Rahman, Egyptian extremists, . . . the Sudanese Islamic Front, and extremist parliamentarians from the Jordanian Islamic Action Front," he wrote. "The real challenge for moderates like myself is to prevent my Muslim brethren from being deceived by extremist groups that pretend to represent their interests."

Ashmawy did more than just expose media spokesmen and argue for a more moderate and tolerant version of Islam. He also tried to warn the U.S. government about the spread of terrorism to its shores. In his Senate testimony he stated,

> Indeed, what I have discovered is that the heart, if not the soul, of the extremists is in fact largely in the United States, where these radicals have set up many of their fund-raising and political headquarters. These groups have literally hijacked the mainstream Islamic organizations here in the United States. They are the engines that drive the radical groups in the Middle East. Besides [providing] millions of dollars of funds as well as propaganda, these groups do something far more dangerous: they provide legitimacy to the radicals.

Tragically, Ashmawy died in a car accident in 1998. His courageous voice will always be missed.

*   *   *

My final example of a hero is also a close friend. Khalid Duran—the colleague with whom I went to Pakistan—has been my friend for many, many years. He is a Muslim and a thoughtful scholar with wide-ranging interests, and a sensitive and humane individual. Perhaps it shouldn't be surprising that there is also a price on his head in the Muslim world.

Duran was born in Spain of parents who were descended from the Barbary pirates of Morocco. "Whenever my children ask about our origins I tell them 'You don't want to know,' " he says. "But when I did tell them my youngest daughter thought it was kind of exciting. 'Now I can be Captain Hook on Halloween,' she said."

Duran lost his father at four but his mother worked doubly hard in bringing him up. Using a wide network of friends and relatives throughout Europe, she helped him get a good education. In 1956 he was sent to live with Hafiz Kamil Silajdzic, a family friend in Bosnia. "They had a ten-year-old son named Haris," says Duran. "I was six years older but we became pretty good friends." Forty years later, Haris Silajdzic became the prime minister of Bosnia, serving from 1993 to 2000, when he resigned in a dispute over how big a part religion should play in the government. (He wanted less.)

Fascinated with his culture and devoted to Islam, Khalid went to Pakistan to finish high school. "I studied in one of the madrassehs—the ones you see in the news, where they now teach nothing but the Koran. They've been there all along. It's just that in my day it was a much more liberal education." Duran mastered Urdu, the native language of Pakistan, as well as Arabic. (He already had Spanish and German and would eventually learn English.) "I think my ambition was to be minister of education in some country," he says. "I just never figured out which one."

At twenty-two he returned to Europe and began studying sociology and political science at the Universities of Bonn and Berlin, supporting himself by doing road construction work. He did his Ph.D. dissertation on "The Quest for Muslim Identity," a study of Amhad Amin, a liberal Egyptian reformer of the early twentieth century. While at the universities he was also courted by the Egyptian Muslim Brotherhood. "It was just a very natural thing," he says. "It was a way for Muslims to get together. They didn't ask me to build bombs or perform terrorist acts or anything. Mostly we had a lot of meetings."

Duran enjoyed the company of fellow Muslims but soon began to doubt their ideology. "It didn't ring well in my ears," he says. "I had grown up in Spain with Franco's fascism and after a while I began to say to myself, 'You know, this sounds like the same thing.' It was a very, very narrow point of view. Muslims were the only good people in the world and we were the only good Muslims." After a few years he quietly dropped his participation.

Upon finishing graduate school, he returned to Pakistan to teach at Islamabad University. "At the time Pakistan was still very much under the British influence and everything was taught in English," he says. "I taught in Urdu. I was the first professor ever to do that. I had only learned it in high school but I could speak it better than the natives."

The years from 1968 to 1974 were turbulent, with the breakaway of East Pakistan to become Bangladesh and a brief war with

India. "There were many sects and they were always recruiting me," he recalls. "I tried them all but it never worked out. I'm too undisciplined."

Instead, he began a further exploration of the Muslim world, doing anthropological research on three cultures—the Andalusian Muslims of Spain, the Swahili Muslims of East Africa, and the Hindustani Muslims of northern India. In the process he met his wife, who is East African.

"Islam is a highly flexible religion that has adapted to many local circumstances," he says. "In Spain you can see the influence of Judaism. In East Africa, you see traces of animism. In India, there is a lot of Buddhism in Islam. Each culture is quite different yet each thinks of itself as the true Islam."

With his broad-based background, Duran began to serve as an ambassador of moderate Islam in many European forums—especially after the Iranian Revolution brought Islamic fundamentalism to the fore. In 1978 he wrote *The Political Role of Islam* for the German Middle East Institute. Among other things, he pointed out the catastrophe that was being caused by Saudi oil money spreading Wahhabism throughout the Muslim world. For this effort he was blacklisted by the Saudi Embassy.

"The fundamentalism of the last half-century is a stranger to traditional Islam," he says. "It's based on something entirely different. Basically, it's a revolt against the modern world. People in modern societies are very cosmopolitan and tolerant of ethnic and cultural differences. They thrive on them. But fundamentalism tries to establish an ethnic purity and withdraw from cosmopolitan society.

"People don't remember, but the Muslim Brotherhood grew up in Egypt in the 1930s as an imitation of European fascism, which was also a revolt against modernity. In Italy and Germany you had the brownshirts and the blackshirts. In Egypt you had the greenshirts, which was the Muslim Brotherhood. It failed in Europe but survived in Egypt and spread to other parts of the Islamic world."

Duran warns that much of the hatred for America comes from the vast disparity of incomes across the globe. "This isn't just an Islamic thing," he says. "You find resentment of America and its people everywhere where there are poor people. They don't have enough to eat and then they turn on television and see something like 'Dallas' or 'Dynasty.' It's bound to cause resentment. Of course you have to realize that watching a television set in the Third World means sharing it with 20 or 30 other people."

Yet some of the worst anti-Americanism among Muslim fundamentalists comes from people who are often remarkably well educated—engineers, doctors, and even scientists. Duran has an answer for that as well.

"The odd thing about Islamic fundamentalism is that it's always had its strongest appeal among engineers," he says. "There's even a joke about it in Arabic. The words '*al-ikhwan al-muslimun*' mean 'Muslim Brothers' and '*al-ikhwan al-muhandisun*' means 'Engineer Brothers.' In Egypt they always say the Muslim Brotherhood is really the Engineering Brotherhood."

Duran attributes this to shortcomings in education. "Engineers don't exercise their fantasy and imagination. Everything is precise and mathematical. They don't study what we call 'the humanities.' Consequently when it comes to issues that involve religion and personal emotion, they tend to see things in very stark terms. The Muslim Brotherhood has become very conscious of this. They've set up special programs in the universities to try to recruit students in the humanities, but they never have any luck. Having an education in literature or politics or sociology seems to inoculate you against the appeals of fundamentalism."

With his broad knowledge and humanistic outlook, Khalid Duran has never had any trouble moving in a multicultured world. His German-language book on Osama bin Laden has been a bestseller in Germany ever since September 11, 2001. In 2001 he also published *Children of Abraham: An Introduction to Islam for Jews* with the American Jewish Committee. The book was endorsed by Prince Hassan of Jordan and received favorable reviews throughout the Muslim world.

Unfortunately, it did not satisfy the Council on American-Islamic Relations in Washington. CAIR wrote a derogatory review, censuring the book's contents and attacking Duran personally, questioning whether he was a "real Muslim." "They referred to me as 'The Pretender,' " he says. "They not only questioned my religion, they doubted my origins and said that Khalid Duran probably wasn't my real name!"

Sheikh 'Abdu-I-Mun'im AbuZant is a mullah with Jordan's Islamic Action Front, that nation's fundamentalist organization. After reading CAIR's review of the book (not the book itself), Sheikh AbuZant called Duran an "apostate" in *Ash-Shahid*, a Jordanian newspaper.[10] Apostasy in Islam is generally regarded as high treason. According to most interpretations of the *shari'a* (law), an apostate from Islam is to be put to death.

Brazenly ignoring reality, CAIR immediately claimed that AbuZant's death threat existed only in the minds of the American Jewish Committee and was a ploy to increase sales of the book.[11] An article in *Az-Zaituna*, the party paper of the Islamic Association of Palestine (IAP), CAIR's parent body, called the *fatwa* concocted, while at the same time dismissing it as unimportant because it had appeared "in a local paper." [12] But in fact the reality was that Duran was now in physical danger.

*   *   *

More than anything else I have experienced in my investigation of Muslim radicalism here and abroad, Khalid Duran's experience proves to me that radical fundamentalists do not represent the real Islam. The breadth of Duran's scholarship and understanding matches that of the great Arab scholars of the Caliphate—the Golden Age of Islam that the fundamentalists look back on with such nostalgia. Yet here when they find the same lofty understanding right in their midst, they reject it and even try to kill it. This is the same book-burning fanaticism that Europe witnessed during the dreadful decade of the 1930s.

I can only hope Muslims everywhere will eventually recognize the self-destructive path that fundamentalism represents and will return to the highest ideals of their true religion.

But in the end, wishing for a "nice" ending to the clash between militant Islam and Islam, we must not blind ourselves to the bitter reality that militant Islamic fundamentalism holds the far more powerful upper hand in the intra-religious debate within Islam. For years prior to September 2001, the West—and the United States in particular—deluded itself into the belief that militant Islamic fundamentalism could be contained, that it was not a strategic threat to the U.S., that it could be co-opted, and that there existed a rigid separation between those groups that "condemned" terrorism and those that engaged in it. The horrific casualties of September 11 showed that our Western conceptions were in fact misconceptions. Militant Islam, in its various incarnations, will continue to be a fixed feature on our political landscape for many years to come.

Appendixes

Appendix A
Current and Recent Militant Islamist Groups in the United States

Seattle, WA
-Algerian Armed Islamic Group

Chicago. N
-Hamas
-Islamic Jihad

San Francisco, CA
-Abu Sayyaf

Santa Clara, CA
-Al Qaeda
-Hamas

Denver, CO
-Al Qaeda

Kansas City, N
-Hamas

Los Angeles, CA
-Hamas
-Al Gama'at al Islamiyya
-Algerian Armed Islamic Group

Oklahoma City, OK
-Hamas (Groups and Conventions)

San Diego, CA
-Algerian Armed Islamic Group

Tucson, AZ
-Al Qaeda
-Hamas

Arlington, TX
-Al Qaeda

Dallas, TX
-Hamas

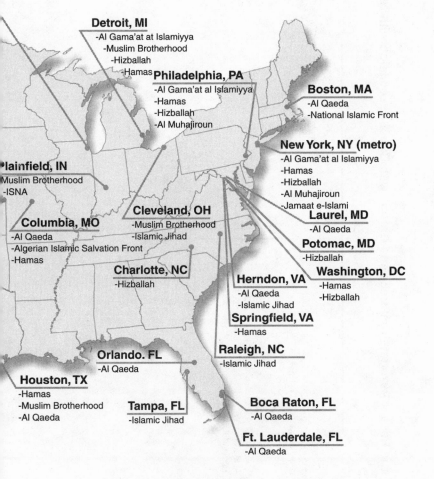

Detroit, MI
-Al Gama'at at Islamiyya
-Muslim Brotherhood
-Hizballah
-Hamas

Philadelphia, PA
-Al Gama'at al Islamiyya
-Hamas
-Hizballah
-Al Muhajiroun

Boston, MA
-Al Qaeda
-National Islamic Front

New York, NY (metro)
-Al Gama'at al Islamiyya
-Hamas
-Hizballah
-Al Muhajiroun
-Jamaat e-Islami

Laurel, MD
-Al Qaeda

Potomac, MD
-Hizballah

Plainfield, IN
-Muslim Brotherhood
-ISNA

Columbia, MO
-Al Qaeda
-Algerian Islamic Salvation Front
-Hamas

Cleveland, OH
-Muslim Brotherhood
-Islamic Jihad

Charlotte, NC
-Hizballah

Herndon, VA
-Al Qaeda
-Islamic Jihad

Washington, DC
-Hamas
-Hizballah

Springfield, VA
-Hamas

Orlando. FL
-Al Qaeda

Raleigh, NC
-Islamic Jihad

Houston, TX
-Hamas
-Muslim Brotherhood
-Al Qaeda

Tampa, FL
-Islamic Jihad

Boca Raton, FL
-Al Qaeda

Ft. Lauderdale, FL
-Al Qaeda

Appendix B
Current and Recent Terrorist Front Cells and Groups with Direct Association with Terrorists

AL QAEDA

Cells: Ft. Lauderdale, FL; Orlando, FL; Boca Raton, FL; Denver, CO;
Laurel, MD; Boston, MA; Columbia, MO; Herndon, VA;
Tucson, AZ; Arlington, TX; Houston, TX

Alkhifa
Refugee Services
Founded in Tucson, AZ, 1986
Ceased major operations, 1994

Major Branch Offices: Arlington, VA; Atlanta, GA; Boulder, CO; Chicago, IL; Clearwater, FL;
Columbia, MO; Dearborn, MI; Jersey City, NJ; Las Cruces, NM; Tucson, AZ;
Lincoln, NE; Los Angeles, CA; Madison, WI; Nashville, TN; New Haven, CT;
Philadelphia, PA; Phoenix, AZ; Portland, OR; Sacramento, CA; Washington, D.C.

Advice and Reformation Committee (ARC)
Incorporated in London, 1994
Kansas City, MO; Denver, CO

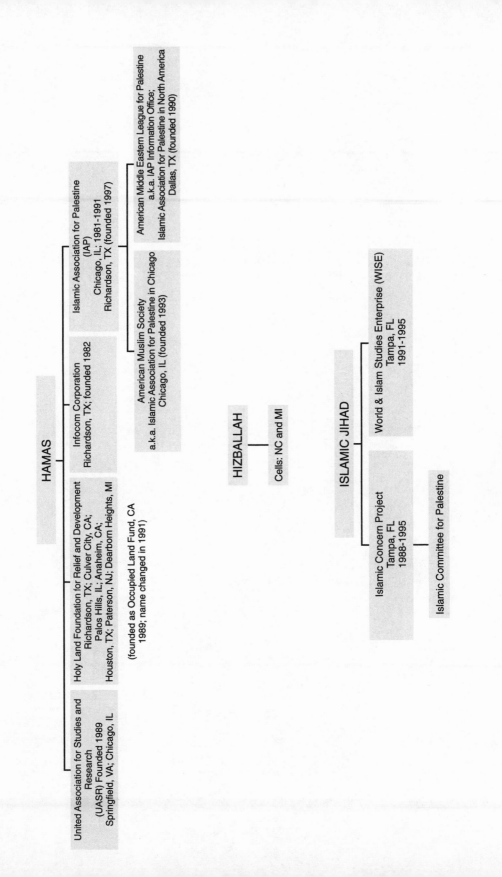

HAMAS

United Association for Studies and Research (UASR) Founded 1989 Springfield, VA; Chicago, IL

Holy Land Foundation for Relief and Development Richardson, TX; Culver City, CA; Palos Hills, IL; Anaheim, CA; Houston, TX; Paterson, NJ; Dearborn Heights, MI

(founded as Occupied Land Fund, CA 1989; name changed in 1991)

Infocom Corporation Richardson, TX; founded 1982

Islamic Association for Palestine (IAP) Chicago, IL; 1981-1991 Richardson, TX (founded 1997)

American Muslim Society a.k.a. Islamic Association for Palestine in Chicago Chicago, IL (founded 1993)

American Middle Eastern League for Palestine a.k.a. IAP Information Office; Islamic Association for Palestine in North America Dallas, TX (founded 1990)

HIZBALLAH

Cells: NC and MI

ISLAMIC JIHAD

Islamic Concern Project Tampa, FL 1988-1995

Islamic Committee for Palestine

World & Islam Studies Enterprise (WISE) Tampa, FL 1991-1995

THE TERRORISTS' SUPPORT NETWORKS

The Sea in Which the Fish Swim

MAYA, AIG, ICW, CAIR, AMC, ICNA, MPAC, AMA, ISNA

Ever since 1993, my staff and I have been investigating militant Islamic networks in the United States. We have attended numerous meetings, making audio and video recordings wherever possible, and we have collected hundreds of thousands of documents, including the publications of various groups.

We have discovered that among prominent groups that enjoy the wide protections granted in this country to "research," "charitable," or "civil-rights" organizations are several who provide significant support for terrorist organizations. All the groups included in this Appendix are radicalized. I have not included any group that accidentally hosted a militant speaker, for example;

what follows is a rundown of groups whose leaders and key activities serve to support and enable terrorist activity, whether through fund-raising, recruitment, or propaganda.

It would be unfair to say these groups are engaged in actual terrorism. But the monies they raise support an entire spectrum of services and activities that support the agenda of radical Islamic ideology. In the United States, militant groups raise financial and military support for their networks in the rest of the world while spreading their *da'wa*—political propaganda—designed to gain adherents. Money is solicited for *zakat* or charity for orphans, widows, and children. But much of this money goes explicitly to support the survivors of "martyrs"—terrorists who have died carrying out acts of violence. Suicide bombers have become common in the Middle East—just as they are now appearing here.

Although all charitable groups deny giving financial support to jihad, monies are commingled when disbursed. In a revealing admission, the *Friday Report,* a militant publication in Colorado, openly stated in 1995 that *zakat* is given for jihad so the "warrior (Mujahid) is equipped and given whatever he needs to fight for the cause of Allah . . . because he is unable to earn his living while fighting." [1] "These groups know money is fungible," says former ambassador Paul Bremer, who served as head of the State Department's Office of Counterterrorism in the 1980s. "Every dollar that is raised to buy milk frees up money that can be poured into terrorist activities."

Although there is no evidence that the myriad Islamic groups in the United States are coordinated centrally, evidence shows an ad hoc collaboration and cross-fertilization among these networks. Sheikh Rahman of Jersey City was sponsored by half a dozen innocent-sounding "charitable" and "religious" organizations while he was plotting to terrorize Manhattan.

MUSLIM ARAB YOUTH ASSOCIATION (MAYA)

Many popular conventions held in the United States have been sponsored by MAYA, which was formed in 1977. MAYA conventions have regularly attracted a parade of top Islamic militants, including Rashid Ghanushi, leader of the Tunisian An-Nahda movement, who has been sentenced to death in Tunisia and now lives in Great Britain; Mustapha Mash'hur, the Supreme Guide of the Egyptian Muslim Brotherhood; Musa Abu Marzook, a top Hamas leader who formerly resided in the United States but who currently lives in Syria; Yusuf al-Qaradawi, an Egyptian Muslim Brotherhood cleric based in Qatar; Ahmad al-Qattan, a radical Hamas leader based in Kuwait; Sheikh Ahmad Nofal, a Hamas recruiter of terrorists in Jordan; and Ibrahim Ghousheh, Hamas's official spokesman. Conferences have been held in Oklahoma City, Chicago, Toledo, Ontario (California), Los Angeles, Detroit, and other cities.

The central tenet of MAYA is that Western society, particularly the United States, is morally corrupt and intrinsically evil. "In the heart of America, in the depths of corruption and ruin and moral deprivation, an elite of Muslim youth is holding fast to the teachings of Allah," states the preface to MAYA's constitution. A companion MAYA publication, "Guide for the Muslim Family in America," does not hide its revulsion for the West: "Western civilization is based upon the separation of religions from life [whereas] Islamic civilization is based upon fundamentals opposed to those of Western civilization." Muslim women are specifically warned to be "conscious of the evils of Western civilization."

MAYA conferences provide social reinforcement to Muslims living in the United States and profess to protect them from secularized Western culture. But they also provide a forum for the expanding militant jihad. "There lies Rome waiting again!" said the welcoming message to MAYA's fifteenth annual convention in Oklahoma City in 1992. The implication, of course, was "an empire waiting to fall." A panoply of radical groups hawked their wares promoting Hamas, the Palestinian Islamic Jihad, and about twenty-five other groups.

These conferences typically have "bazaars" or markets where different organizations set up booths to garner support for their many causes. At the booth for the Islamic Association for Palestine, books extolling the conspiracies between Jews and the United States abounded. When I asked how one could help the cause of Palestine, the young man at the table replied, "First you must understand who our enemies are." Then he handed me a pamphlet entitled "America's Greatest Enemy: The Jew!" Copies of the Hamas charter described the inner workings of the global conspiracy of Jews and Western "crusaders" to destroy Islam.

One of the highlights of the four-day conference was the "Palestine Evening," restricted to Muslims and would-be converts. In his trademark raspy voice, Kamal Helbawi, a leader of the Egyptian Muslim Brotherhood based in Pakistan, delivered a spellbinding address. Two years before, Helbawi had demanded that the borders of Jordan be open "so that Muslim youth can confront the Jews and the Americans at once." On this night he was giving the keynote address. "Oh noble Brothers," he began, "the Palestinian cause is not a conflict over borders and land only. It is not a conflict over thought or human ideology. It is not a conflict over peace alone. Rather it is an absolute clash of civilizations, between truth and falsehood—a conflict between two inclinations, a Satanic inclination led by Jews and their allies and a divine inclination, led by Hamas, the entire Islamic movement, and the Islamic people standing behind them." [2]

Helbawi was followed by Khaled Mishal, a Hamas operative from Sudan, who lauded the "heroism of Hamas fighters." "Since the Muslim nation of Palestine has decided to take matters into its own hands, it has decided to engage in Jihad to reclaim their land of Palestine. This blessed *intifada* was evoked by Sheikh Ahmad Yasin, the weak and paralyzed man who caused the earth to shake under the feet of the occupiers. Since that time the Palestinian people have shown examples of sacrifice and human courage. Among the proof are their Molotov [cocktails] and knives." [3]

After a Hamas "state-of-the-union" report, Mishal asked for contributions from the increasingly emotional crowd, which frequently interrupted with chants of "Allahu akbar!" (Allah is great!). Mishal specifically asked that contributions be given to the Holy Land Foundation for Relief and Development. At the time, I was just back from the Gaza Strip. Listening to all this incendiary invective being spouted in Oklahoma City was a little unreal. The most intense moment came when the crowd of several thousand joined to chant: "Khaybar, Khaybar, ya Yahud; Jay'sh Muhammad saufa ya'ud!" which means "Kaybar, Kaybar, O Jews! The Army of Muhammad Will Return!" This contemporary chant is to remind Jews of Muhammad's victory over them and the annihilation of some of the Jewish tribes in the seventh century of the common era.

Although the Crusades took place 900 years ago, you would think they happened yesterday. From Bosnia to Kashmir, from Palestine to the Philippines to the United States, it is said, Muslims are being subjected to vicious genocidal assaults that require the response of militant Islamic youth. The reaction of MAYA's Arabic newspaper to my video was "Jihad in America: The Crusades Continue!"

Men and women are kept separate at MAYA conferences, although they mix in the halls and elevators. Almost all the women wear traditional Muslim headscarves. Half the attendants are younger than twenty, a microcosm of the dramatic demographic changes in the Muslim world. In 1995 in Toledo the mood of the gathering was upbeat. Islamic fundamentalists had scored big victories in Egypt and Algeria. In the Philippines rebels had made dramatic gains. The siege of Muslims in Bosnia and Chechnya only served to reinforce the charge that the crusades persisted. Finally, in Palestine, Hamas suicide attacks had once again penetrated the Zionist enemy in his very home.

Two floors below was a mass-market bazaar of Muslim paraphernalia. Sprinkled throughout were books on Jews. One (still available) was entitled "The Struggle for Existence Between the Quran and the Talmud." It described in methodical detail the evil traits and subhuman qualities of Jews, routinely referring to them as "children of snakes" and "descendants of apes." Another was an Arabic translation of a Nazi publication, updated to include evils committed by Jews against Muslims. A children's coloring book in Arabic featured caricatures of evil-looking, hook-nosed bearded characters emblazoned with Jewish stars. Several editions of the "Protocols of the Elders of Zion," along with "Freemasons and Christians Conspiracy Against Islam" and "The Myth of Jesus Christ" adorned the shelves.

The Committee to Free Sheikh Omar Abdel Rahman did a brisk business collecting donations for the imprisoned mullah. "U.S. War on Islam and Its Scholars" proclaimed the brochure of the American Islamic Group in San Diego. The sheik's indictment, the pamphlet proclaimed, was a "prelude for a U.S. government campaign against all Muslim activists." It was "proof that Islam in America is targeted by the U.S. government. After four of the brothers were convicted in the WTC bombing, the court marshals threw the Qurans that the brothers were holding on the floor and then stepped on it [sic]. They said, 'Call Allah to help you now!' This is a case against Islam and not against these 16 Muslims." Another broadside called for the reinstatement of the Islamic Caliphate and condemned the "evil systems of capitalism and democracy."

But the main attraction at MAYA conferences was the charismatic speakers. Kamal Helbawi has been a perennial favorite. At MAYA's 1994 meeting about killing women and children with car bombs, he responded, "Children will grow up to be Golda Meir or Shimon Peres." Bassam al-Amoush, who at the time was a leader of the Islamic bloc in the Jordanian Parliament, opined,

"Once in a mosque, somebody asked me, 'If I see a Jew on the street, should I kill him?' I said, 'Don't ask me. After you kill him come and tell me.'" The crowd roared with laughter. "What do you want from me, a *fatwa* [religious ruling]?" he persisted. "A good deed does not require one."[4]

Minutes later a messenger interrupted al-Amoush's lecture, handing another speaker a note. A hush fell over the conference room. "We have good news," the speaker proclaimed. "A Palestinian policeman has carried out a suicide bombing in Jerusalem. Three were killed and fifteen wounded. Hamas claims responsibility for the incident." The crowd responded ecstatically with shouts of "Takbir! Allahu akbar! Allahu akbar!"[5]

At the 1997 MAYA conference held in Ontario, California, Egyptian cleric Sheikh Wagdy Ghuneim made a presentation. In his speech, Sheikh Ghuneim, in reference to four suicide bombings that took place in Israel in 1996, stated, "Those young people who explode themselves to kill the Jews were not committing suicide but jihad. They are mujahideen because there is no way to struggle and fight the Jews except that way. Allah bless those martyrs."[6]

THE AMERICAN ISLAMIC GROUP (AIG)

The American Islamic Group (AIG), a now-defunct organization formerly based in San Diego, California, described itself as a "nonprofit, non-sectarian, religious service institution primarily established to protect the rights of Muslims and to provide economic, humanitarian, educational assistance" to needy Muslims.[7] Whatever its humanitarian and civil rights-oriented activities, the AIG was in fact an extremely radical Islamic organization, dedicated to destroying infidel states around the world. The rationale behind the AIG's mission was simple: "Since the establishment of the rule of Allah is the necessary prerequisite to fulfilling the final duty of judgment and government, its establishment is, of course, obligatory."[8] Its chief publication, the *Islam Report,* made for chilling reading.

Aside from its own publications, the AIG disseminated communiqués of Middle Eastern terrorist organizations. One of the most radical groups endorsed by the American Islamic Group was the GIA, a terrorist organization whose *raison d'être* is the overthrow of the "un-Islamic government" of Algeria. The American Islamic Group served as a distribution center in the United States for such GIA publications as *Al-Murabitoun, Al-Qital,* and *Sawt Al-Jihad.*[9] According to the American Islamic Group, the GIA is "the only legitimate leadership of Muslim resistance in Algeria."[10] Reports of the numerous atrocities committed by the GIA appeared daily on the *Islam Report*—including a particularly gruesome attack in which GIA members kidnapped and decapitated seven French monks. Algeria has been one of the bloodiest battlegrounds in the world in recent decades, with militant Islamic rebels and the secular military government slaughtering tens of thousands in their struggle with one another. Anwar Haddam, the leader of Algeria's Islamic Salvation Front, allied with the GIA, attempted to obtain political asylum here in 1993. Though the Immigration and Naturalization Service (INS) determined in December 1996 that he had been directly involved in promoting acts of terrorism and refused his asylum request, Haddam has since been released from INS custody and is currently residing in the northern Virginia suburbs of Washington, D.C.

Elsewhere, AIG supported the Chechens in their war against the Russians. During the war in 1995, AIG published appeals from the Islamist Chechen president, Dzhokar Dudayev, for 10,000 Muslims to join the war against Russian troops.[11] Likewise, AIG published statements from *Harakat Al Jihad Al Islami Al Eretri* (the Eritrean Islamic Jihad Movement) claiming responsibility for ambushes, assassinations, and a number of antigovernment military operations in Eritrea.[12] Members of the Eritrean Islamic Jihad are reported to have been trained by Osama bin Laden's al Qaeda organization.[13]

Perhaps most troubling of all was the AIG's endorsement of the Committee for the Defense of Legitimate Rights (CDLR), a militant fundamentalist Saudi opposition group devoted to overthrowing the current Islamic regime in Saudi Arabia. CDLR is extremely radical in its views. In an interview in 1996, CDLR spokesman Mohammad al-Mas'ari said "the battle against the Jews is a specific obligation on all Muslims until they annihilate them and drive them out of Palestine . . . they must be fought until they are exterminated."[14] In the April/May 1994 *Islam Report*, AIG stated, "The American Islamic Group urges every good Muslim to support his brother at CDLR, and provide them all the help necessary in the accomplishment of their just cause [i.e., the overthrow of the government of Saudi Arabia]. AIG announces that it is putting all its resources and strength in supporting our brothers Drs. al-Mas'ari and al-Faqih at CDLR." Two years later, on March 18, 1996, the sentiment was repeated: "The American Islamic Group salutes with brotherhood and love their brothers Dr. Mohammad al-Mas'ari and Dr. Ad'ad al-Faqeeh for their courageous stands in the fact of this test and we are very pleased that the enemies of Allah failed to destroy the righteous Islamic movement for reform in the land of Islam . . . the American Islamic Group is behind you both."

The head of the American Islamic Group (AIG) in the United States was Kifah W. Jayyousi. Jayyousi lived in the San Diego area until approximately 1996 or 1997, at which time he relocated to Detroit.[15] In July 1999 Jayyousi was hired as the District of Columbia School Systems facilities director.[16] He left that position in April 2001.

ISLAMIC CULTURAL WORKSHOP (ICW)

During the 1990s, one little-known West Coast organization spread the call of Islamic extremism by means of publications and videos. The Islamic Cultural Workshop (ICW) was based in Walnut, California from as early as 1992 to as recently as 1999. Today it appears to be largely inactive. Its primary publications were a bi-monthly newsletter named *Khalif'ornia*—a juxtaposition of the words "Khilifah" or Islamic State (sometimes Anglicized as "caliphate") and "California"—and a quarterly magazine named the *Khalif'ornia Journal.* The ICW set up booths at various Islamic conferences throughout the United States where they sold both publications, in addition to books and videos espousing the views of its Middle Eastern parent organization, Hizb-ut-Tahrir, or the Party of Liberation. At the 1998 conference of the Muslim Arab Youth Association (MAYA), for example, the ICW was busy hawking a book by the founder of Hizb-ut-Tahrir, Taqiuddin an-Nabhani, entitled *The Islamic State.*

Hizb-ut-Tahrir was founded in Jerusalem in 1953, by Sheikh Taqiuddin an-Nabhani, a Jordanian who studied theology at Egypt's Al Azhar University. The philosophy of Hizb-ut-Tahrir is simple and extremely militant: "Muslims nowadays live in Dar al-Kufr [the World of Infidels]."[17] To Hizb-ut-Tahrir, this situation is intolerable—the only solution to the problem is for Muslims to reestablish the *Khilafah,* or Islamic State.[18] Toward that end, the organization has been implicated in attempted or planned acts of terrorism in the 1980s and 1990s.

Hizb-ut-Tahrir is striving to "resume the Islamic way of life and to convey the Islamic *da'wa* [message] to the world. . . . It also aims to bring back the Islamic guidance for mankind and to lead the *Ummah* [Islamic community] into a struggle with *Kufr* [infidels], its systems and its thoughts so that Islam encapsulates the world."[19] According to Hizb-ut-Tahrir, the *Khilafah,* or Islamic State, does not currently exist anywhere in the world. Iran and Sudan do not qualify; the *Khilafah* is one large Islamic State, ruled by a single leader (called a 'Caliph') *without* national boundaries.

Theoretically speaking, the *Khilafah* would be governed solely by Islamic law; it would be neither liberal nor democratic. Hizb-ut-Tahrir makes it clear what this society would be like when it states that "The four common 'freedoms' [belief, speech, ownership of capital, and personal freedom] are in conflict with the laws of Islam." [20]

To Hizb-ut-Tahrir, the *Khilafah* is not something that is optional. It is commanded by Islam, as Muhammad said: " 'Whosoever dies without having a *bay'ah* [pledge of allegiance] to the *Khilafah* [Islamic State] upon his neck, dies a death of *jahiliyyah* [ignorance]' . . . a failure to observe this duty is a negligence of one of the most important commands of Islam." [21]

Taqiuddin an-Nabhani had a very clear vision of what had to be accomplished in order to realize the goal of *Khilafah*. As in 7th-century Mecca when the survival of the fledgling Islamic community depended on individual sacrifice and total submission to Allah, the realization of *Khilafah*, for an-Nabhani, will be based on the degree to which the Muslim community is willing to sacrifice. The endeavor will fail without jihad [holy war]. In his book *Islamic Concepts*, an-Nabhani maintained that "[J]ihad is the established method (which is unchangeable) for spreading Islam." For an-Nabhani, there was no alternative but jihad: "Jihad is to call to Islam and to fight for the sake of Allah. . . . Jihad *is fard* [compulsory]." [22]

When the Muslims get the upper hand, according to an-Nabhani, the Koran will dictate the course of events: ". . . if the enemies from the *kafireen* [infidels] are encircled then they will be invited to Islam. . . . If they rejected Islam, then *Jiziya* [tribute] would be demanded from them . . . if the enemy rejected Islam and rejected paying the *jiziya* then it is *Halal* [permissible] to fight against them." [23]

Since its inception, Hizb-ut-Tahrir has been based primarily in Jordan and Lebanon. It has existed in relative obscurity except for a brief few moments: in 1981, members of the organization staged a failed assault on the military academy in Alexandria, Egypt; in 1988, group members attempted a coup d'etat in Tunisia; and in 1993 members were accused of plotting to overthrow King Hussein of Jordan.[24]

Consistent with its support for terrorists, in 1988, Hizb-ut-Tahrir published a treatise entitled "The Islamic Rule on Hijacking Aeroplanes," which sanctioned the hijacking of aircraft of countries considered to be against Muslims. Needless to say, according to Hizb-ut-Tahrir, the United States qualifies as an enemy of Islam: "The system of Islam is the only real threat that America faces, and the [American] conspiracy to destroy Islam is proof of that threat. As Muslims we should realize that only we as an *Ummah* [community] have the potential to not only counter the American plans, but also to take Islam to the rest of the world."[25]

For the ICW, *Khalif'ornia* and the *Khalif'ornia Journal* provided a forum for the dissemination of the ideology of Hizb ut-Tahrir within the United States. As stated in the *Khalif'ornia Journal,* "Hizb ut-Tahrir is the first Islamic Movement since the demise of the Islamic State that is seriously willing to enter society."[26] In editions of the *Khalif'ornia Journal* from January 1996 through June 1997, "A Draft Constitution of the Islamic State," a document prepared by Hizb-ut-Tahrir was published in its entirety.

Regarding what they referred to as the "butcherization from the Muslims in Bosnia," the pages of *Khalif'ornia* stated, "Help them by not carrying candles [in peaceful vigils]. Muslims need swords, not candles!"[27] Against whom these swords might be used was further explained: "The *Khilafah* would regard states with imperialistic motives, such as the United States, Britain, and Russia, as belligerent and potential enemies of war. . . . [S]tates such as Israel . . . would be regarded as actual enemies of war." [28]

In another article entitled "Qaid'a: A Legal Principle," the use of weapons in Islam is explained: "Use of Swords is permissible in Islam, however, what Islam restricts is the way it is utilized. . . . [T]he act of using a sword in Jihad is rewarded." [29]

Not surprisingly, the Islamic Cultural Workshop was violently opposed to the Israeli-Palestinian peace agreements: "All the current peace treaties with Israel [are forbidden]. . . . The treaties are an oppressively clear infringement upon the rights and interests of Muslims. They also run against the interests of Islam and the goals of the foreign policy in Islam." [30]

The absolute goal of the Islamic Cultural Workshop, the re-establishment of the Islamic State, requires combat with all infidel Jewish and Christian societies. What the establishment of this Islamic State means to those in the West is a repeat of the history of the Islamic State, i.e., "the Islamic State carried Islam to the world through *da'wa* [propagation] and jihad to expand the horizons of Islamic rule." [31]

THE COUNCIL ON AMERICAN-ISLAMIC RELATIONS (CAIR)

CAIR is the most prominent of the Muslim organizations concerned with "civil rights." In its charter, CAIR stated it would "promote interest and understanding among the general public with regards to Islam and Muslims in North America and conduct educational services in the fields of religion, culture, education, society and history concerning Islamic issues both in the United States and abroad." The organization generally purports to represent the Muslim viewpoint in America.

Founded in 1994, CAIR is an outgrowth of the Islamic Association of Palestine. In 1994, then-IAP president Omar Ahmad approached Nihad Awad, IAP's public relations director, and "suggested that they leave the IAP and concentrate on combating anti-Muslim discrimination nationwide."[32] When the organization was incorporated, the three individuals involved were Awad, Ahmad, and Rafiq Jaber who served as Ahmad's successor to the position of president of the IAP.

CAIR takes the public position that it condemns terror. Shortly after the events of September 11, 2001, the organization took out a full-page advertisement in *The Washington Post* stating: "We at the Council on American Islamic Relations, along with the entire American Muslim Community, are deeply saddened by the massive loss of life resulting from the tragic events of September 11th. American Muslims unequivocally condemn these vicious and cowardly acts of terrorism. . . . We join all Americans in calling for the swift apprehension and punishment of the perpetrators of these crimes."

On its Web site, the statement appears as an adjunct to a section labeled "Passenger Profiling," in which American Muslims are invited to submit complaints "if you or someone you know has been a victim." Another subsection titled "Help for Victims" asks, "What you can do for the victims of the WTC and Pentagon attacks" and allows contributions through both the Red Cross and the Holy Land Foundation.

In fact CAIR has often served as an ideological support group for militants. On May 24, 1998, for example, CAIR cosponsored an incendiary rally at Brooklyn College that featured speakers spouting anti-Jewish rhetoric. One speaker was Wagdy Ghuneim, a radical cleric from Egypt. He told listeners, "Allah says he who equips a warrior of jihad is like the one makes jihad himself." He led the audience in a song with the lyrics: "No to the Jews, descendants of the apes." [33]

On October 28, 1998, CAIR's Southern California branch issued a press release to protest the existence of billboards in the Los Angeles area that depicted the visage of Osama bin Laden with the headline "the sworn enemy." The billboards had been sponsored by the Los Angeles-based KCOP Television, Inc., and were intended "to take recognizable characters and situations that affect people's lives because they are in the news" (as CAIR put it).[34] The CAIR statement claimed that the billboard was "an insult to the hundreds of thousands of Muslims who live in Southern California." [35]

CAIR has even refused to condemn the Taliban. A conference in Columbus, Ohio, entitled "Leadership Ambassadors, Making a Difference," featured a seminar led by CAIR's Director of Communications, Ibrahim Hooper. There, Hooper explained how he preferred to contextualize the regime:

> [O]ften I'm dealing with very sensitive controversial issues, and I don't want to be quoted about the Taliban, you know, but I want to put the Taliban into context for a reporter. So I'll say well, you know, CAIR doesn't comment on international issues where there is not an

American component so we just don't have any comment. But, can we go off the record, and then I'll go off the record in trying to explain what is going on so that they don't just go away with a stereotypical, one dimensional portrayal. . . ."[36]

CAIR's executive director, Nihad Awad, explained his views regarding the Palestinian situation in a speech delivered in 1994 at Barry University in Florida: "After I researched the situation inside and outside Palestine, I am in support of the Hamas movement. . . ."[37] In 2000 Awad appeared at a rally in front of the White House in Washington, D.C., and rejected any peaceful settlement between the Israelis and the Palestinians: "they [the Jews] have been saying 'Next year in Jerusalem'—we say 'Next year to all Palestine.' "[38] He also stated that Hollywood had distorted its treatment of groups engaged in violence in the Middle East by referring to them as terrorists: "Hollywood is not our friend. Hollywood has distorted the facts. Hollywood has shown freedom fighters as terrorists. Hollywood has done the work that Zionists cannot done [sic]."[39]

CAIR officials have defended the action of suicide bombers. On the one hand, Awad told CNN's "Crossfire" that "Suicide is an act of disbelief, because we Muslims believe that God is only in charge of life and death. And to take one's life or other people's life is an act of disbelief and it goes in sharp contradiction with Islamic teachings."[40] On the other hand, at a conference of the Islamic Association for Palestine held a week later, Omar Ahmad, chairman of CAIR's board of directors, told a youth session: "Someone in

Islam is allowed to fight. . . . Fighting for freedom, fighting for Islam—that is not suicide. They kill themselves for Islam." [41]

Much of CAIR's time is spent trying to persuade the press not to "overreact" to acts of Muslim terror and trying to prove that Muslims themselves are victims of discrimination and prejudice. A year after the bombings of the American embassies in Kenya and Tanzania in 1998 that killed 224 people, Jeff Jacoby of *The Boston Globe* wrote: "On that occasion, prominent Islamic voices in the United States *did* speak out. But their chief message was not one of horrified sympathy for the victims and their families or of shame that anyone calling himself a Muslim could perpetrate such an atrocity. No—what [these] Muslim leaders were eager to communicate was a warning to the media not to speculate about a possible Islamic connection to the slaughter.

"A release issued by the Council on American-Islamic Relations was typical: 'American Muslims Ask Journalists to Exercise Restraint in Reporting on Embassy Bombings,' ran the headline. At the time, despite the ferocity of those bombings, America's major Islamic groups made no move to distance themselves from bin Laden—or even to label him a terrorist." [42]

CAIR has several ties to the Hamas-connected organizations and individuals discussed in Chapter 5. At its founding, CAIR received funding of $5,000 from the Holy Land Foundation for Relief and Development. According to annual reports filed in the state of Illinois, Mohammad Nimer, the director of CAIR's Research Center, was on the Board of Directors of the United Association for Studies and Research (UASR). After September 11, 2001, and up until the U.S. government froze the assets of the Holy Land

Foundation in December, CAIR's Web site included a feature, "What you can do for the victims of the WTC and Pentagon attacks," with a link to the Web site of HLF ("Donate through the Holy Land Foundation").

When Federal Judge Kevin Duffy ordered the extradition of Hamas leader Mousa abu Marzook in 1996, CAIR coordinated a press conference on May 10 to protest the decision. CAIR also signed a letter, printed in a June 1996 "Newsletter of the Marzuk [sic] Legal Fund," arguing that the extradition order was "anti-Islamic" and "anti-American."

Steve Pomerantz, former chief of the Counterterrorism Section of the FBI and former assistant director of the FBI, says: "CAIR has defended individuals involved in terrorist violence, including Hamas leader Musa abu Marzook. . . . The modus operandi has been to falsely tar as 'anti-Muslim' the U.S. government, counter-terrorist officials, writers, journalists and others who have investigated or exposed the threat of Middle East–based terrorism. . . . Unfortunately, CAIR is but one of the new generation of new groups in the United States that hide under a veneer of 'civil rights' or 'academic' status but in fact are tethered to a platform that supports terrorism."

Seif Ashmawy, former publisher of *Voice of Peace,* wrote: "It is a known fact that both the AMC and CAIR have defended, apologized for and rationalized the actions of extremist groups and leaders such as convicted World Trade Center conspirator Sheikh Omar Abdul Rahman, Egyptian extremists, Hassan al-Turabi, the Sudanese National Islamic Front, and extremist parliamentarians from the Jordanian Islamic Action Front and others who called for the overthrow of the Egyptian government. . . . As a proud American Muslim . . . I bow to no one on my defense of Muslim civil rights, but CAIR . . . champion[s] extremists whose views do not represent Islam."

THE AMERICAN MUSLIM COUNCIL (AMC)

The American Muslim Council (AMC) was established as a tax-exempt organization in July of 1990 to "educate [the] public about Muslims."[44] The AMC, in fact, supports radical Islamist causes. Its leaders have openly championed Hamas terrorists, defended Middle Eastern terrorist regimes, issued anti-Semitic and anti-American statements. The AMC supports "the worst, most vicious and most radical terrorist movements and regimes in the Middle East and Africa," says Michael D. Horowitz, Director of the Hudson Institute's Project for Civil Justice Reform.

The AMC is a founder, corporate parent and supporter of several militant Islamic groups including: American Muslims for Jerusalem, a militant group that routinely invokes "Zionist" conspiracies and has featured calls at its conferences for the killing of Jews; and the Kosovo Task Force, an organization that has promoted jihad around the globe, including in "Palestine," and has condemned the seizure by the FBI of funds in Chicago used to support the radical Hamas terrorist organization as an "attack on Muslim civil rights."

The AMC served as the headquarters of the U.S. office of the Islamic Salvation Front (FIS), a militant fundamentalist group whose U.S.-based representative was jailed pending deportation proceedings for his support of terrorism. The AMC has aggressively attacked Sheikh Muhammad Hisham Kabbani, a leading moderate voice in the American Muslim community (see Chapter 8).

The AMC has also spoken out against counter-terrorism legislation as being a product of the Jewish influence on American policy. In 1995, in reference to an executive order and to a bill proposed by President Clinton, then-AMC President Mohammed Cheema stated, "It is now well known that this Executive Order, and the Omnibus Anti-Terrorist legislation proposed by the White House a few days later, are the result of intense Jewish pressure on the White House. With Bill Clinton being frequently regarded as a one-term president, it is expedient to secure Jewish political support for 1996." [45]

According to Nazir Khaja, who resigned as chairman of the Board of Directors and president of AMC, no one in the organization really knows "where the funds for AMC are coming from, how are they being raised and spent, and who is actually controlling this whole process." Khaja explained, "It has been repeatedly brought up that the money is being raised abroad in the Middle East by one person, Mr. Abdulrahman al-Amoudi, who has built contacts overseas only in the name of, and because of, AMC, and who chooses to dispense with it as he pleases with no knowledge or approval of the Board. These are serious concerns, which have the potential for damage to not only just AMC, but also the possibility of severe collateral damage to the overall image and the efforts of the American Muslim community." [46]

The AMC has routinely featured or honored Islamic militants or supporters of terrorism at its annual conferences. At its 1997 convention, the AMC hosted Layth Shubaylat,[47] a terrorist implicated in an Islamic plot to topple the regime of then-King Hussein in Jordan.[48] Shubaylat has managed a legal defense fund for Ahmed Daqamisa, the Jordanian soldier convicted in the killing of Israeli schoolgirls in Naharayim in 1997.[49] In early 1995, AMC hosted a visit by Dr. Yusuf al-Qaradawi. Al-Qaradawi, a renowned Muslim cleric, has blessed "martyrdom operations in which a given Muslim fighter turns himself or herself into a human bomb that casts terror in the hearts of the enemy. . . . If we can't carry out acts of Jihad ourselves, we at least should support and prop up the mujahideen financially and morally so that they will be steadfast until God's victory."[50]

At its 1998 National Convention, the AMC hosted Dr. Sami al-Arian, who is under investigation by the FBI and the INS for his role with WISE and ICP in Tampa, Florida (see Chapter 6). On August 30, 2000, the INS showed a videotape during bond redetermination proceedings which showed al-Arian stating, "Let us damn America. Let us damn Israel, let us damn their allies until death. Why do we stop?" In another segment al-Arian refers to Jews as "monkeys and pigs" and states, "Mohammad is leader. The Koran is our constitution. Jihad is our path. Victory to Islam. Death to Israel. Revolution! Revolution! Until Victory! Rolling, rolling to Jerusalem."

At the 1999 AMC Convention, the organization bestowed annual "awards" on the Holy Land Foundation for Relief and Development (HLF). It also honored the *Washington Report on Middle East Affairs,* a publication that routinely invokes Jewish conspiracies and champions Islamic extremism. Its editors, Richard Curtiss and Andrew Killgore, have been featured speakers before the Liberty Lobby, labeled by the Anti-Defamation League as the most active anti-Semitic organization in the United States.[51]

The AMC has cosponsored conferences tgether with the United Association for Studies and Research (UASR). AMC's Abdulrahman Alamoudi has served on the Board of Directors of UASR. On UASR's 1997 annual report filed with the state of Illinois, where it is incorporated, Aly Abuzaakouk, AMC's president, was listed as president of UASR.

On October 28, 2000, pro-Palestinian protesters marched from Freedom Plaza to Lafayette Park in Washington, D.C., singing "Victory comes from Allah and Hizballah is our model" and "Oh dear Nasrallah, we are allied with you in liberation." On arriving at Lafayette Park, a rally commenced that included Abdulrahman Alamoudi, former AMC executive director and now secretary of AMC's Board of Directors. Alamoudi addressed the cheering crowd:

"I have been labeled by the media in New York to be a supporter of Hamas. Anybody supports Hamas here? [*Crowd cheers responsively.*] Anybody is a supporter of Hamas here? [*Crowd repeats cheer.*] Anybody is a supporter of Hamas here? [*Crowd cheers even louder.*] Hear that, Bill Clinton? We are ALL supporters of Hamas. Allahu akbar! [*Crowd cheers.*] I wish they added that I am also a supporter of Hizballah ... anybody supports Hizballah here? [*Crowd cheers responsively.*]"[52]

At the end of January 2001 in Beirut, the same Abdulrahman Alamoudi attended and participated in what the U.S. State Department called a terrorist conference with a "destructive agenda."[53] The conference brought together leaders of Hamas, Hizballah, Islamic Jihad, and Osama bin Laden's organization. The communiqué issued at the end of the conference stated, "The only decisive option to achieve this strategy [the destruction of Israel] is the option of Jihad in all its forms and resistance. . . . " The communiqué also called for a boycott of American products (in addition to Israeli products): "The American products are exactly like the Israeli products. America today is a second Israel."[54]

ISLAMIC CIRCLE OF NORTH AMERICA (ICNA)

Formally established in 1971, the Islamic Circle of North America (ICNA) is composed primarily of Muslim supporters of South Asian descent. It is allied with the militant fundamentalist movement of Jamaat-e-Islamiya in Pakistan and Bangladesh.

ICNA openly supports militant Islamic fundamentalist organizations, praises terrorist attacks, issues incendiary attacks on Western values and policies, and supports the imposition of the *shar'ia* (Islamic code of law). It has created several nonprofit charitable organizations that collect tax-deductible contributions for militant Islamic causes. ICNA's views are disseminated through regular conferences and a monthly publication called *The Message*.

In March of 1996, Senator Mitch McConnell (R-KY), chairman of the Foreign Operations subcommittee of the Senate Committee on Appropriations, stated that "One of the groups with

Hamas ties is the Dallas-based Islamic Association for Palestine in North America, which, in turn, apparently is allied with the Islamic Circle of North America in New York."

According to an ICNA brochure, *da'wa* (proselytizing) is an integral function of the organization: "ICNA invites both Muslims and non-Muslims to understand Islam (the only way of life prescribed by Allah) as a complete code of life and to enter into its fold totally."[55] Objective 5 in the brochure states ICNA's pledge "to make every effort to contact, cooperate with, and coordinate the Islamic movements outside North America."[56]

In 1995, ICNA's president made the following comments on the topic of jihad at a conference in Columbus, Ohio: "Sometimes, especially nowadays, I hear some Muslims defining jihad, and they will talk and talk and talk about everything in jihad, but they'll be very careful that there is nothing of *qital* [battle, fight, combat] mentioned in there. Well, at least you should not be disrespectful to the people you're talking to. They can pick up a Koran of any translation, and see whatever is there in an instant. And a strong part of Islam is *qital*, and all nations and all people have a legitimate use of violence and war. And in Islam we came up with the first international law, that when you have *qital*, then you have 'culture of *qital*.' There's a method, there's a decision-making body. It's not that a person gets angry and he starts his own *qital*. But when you present jihad you have to present it in its entirety."[57]

At a 1989 Kansas City conference sponsored by the Islamic Association for Palestine, Sayid Thaqib, an ICNA representative, came to express the organization's solidarity with Hamas. At one point Thaqib told the gathering: "We say to the enemies of Islam, wherever they may be, that their days are limited, and they will have no refuge after we show them true Islam, and there is no peace without Islam. And this message we send to all Muslims, and especially the mujahideen in Palestine, and if we are not with you in our bodies, then we are with you in our in our hearts, through our material and activist support, praised be Allah. And we assert to you that the Dawn of Islam is coming in Palestine, and we will see it *in sha Ullah* in Palestine, and all the Islamic countries, and Allah bless them with true Islam *in sha Ullah.*"[60]

From July 6 to 8, 2001, in Cleveland, Ohio, ICNA held its 26th annual convention under the title "Islam for Peace and Justice: Palestine, Kashmir, and Imam Jamil." As part of a fundraising dinner, ICNA member Munir el-Kassem, from Canada, urged the organization's supporters to make a donation of $10,000 each towards ICNA because "We need to accumulate enough with actions to deserve to go home safely. And we know what I mean by home, not the home of this *dunya* (this world), but the home that we all yearn for: the home of *al-Akhira* (the next world). If you really want to have that you should do jihad with your wealth."

The previous year's ICNA convention was held from June 30 to July 2, 2000, in Baltimore, and featured the leader of Pakistan's Jamaat-e-Islamiya, Ameer Qazi Hussain Ahmad. The Jamaat-e-Islamiya is the most prominent radical Islamic movement in Pakistan and its members openly support the Taliban government and learn the ways of jihad. At the conference, Ameer Ahmad alleged that the principal duty of American Muslims is to unite in a single government with Muslims all over the world: "Now, this is the duty of the American Muslims, the Muslims living here, they have got a message. The Muslims everywhere are with a message. . . . We have got a universal message and we are a universal government." [59]

THE MUSLIM PUBLIC AFFAIRS COUNCIL (MPAC)

The Muslim Public Affairs Council (MPAC) was founded in 1988 as a nonprofit social welfare organization with a 501(c)(4) tax status. MPAC calls itself a "public service agency working for the civil rights of American Muslims, for the integration of Islam into American pluralism, and for a positive, constructive relationship between American Muslims and their representatives." [60] While these objectives reflect magnanimous intentions, MPAC's many rallies and sponsored events reveal implicit support of terrorist activities.

On October 28, 2000, MPAC was a cosponsor of a rally in Washington, D.C. in support of the recent spate of violence known as the Al-Aqsa *intifada* between the Palestinians and the Israelis. (This was the rally at which the American Muslim Council's Abdulrahman Alamoudi exhorted the crowd to voice their support for the Hamas and Hizballah terrorist organizations.) During these exhortations, MPAC's Political Advisor, Mahdi Bray, stood directly behind Alamoudi and was seen jubilantly exclaiming his support for these two deadly terrorist organizations. Dr. Maher Hathout, MPAC's Senior Advisor, also participated in this rally. Later, in an article in *The American Muslim*, rather than condemning the rally for its extremist and militant views, Hathout heralded the rally as a marker of a "new era": "The rally in Washington, D.C.

was the embodiment of this new phase of activism in the United States. . . . [T]he speakers and the slogans were relevant and pertinent to the American seen [sic] . . . It was then not a normal rally . . . it transcended the barriers and limitations of a specific local struggle. . . . It is a new era . . ."[61]

Maher Hathout condemned the U.S. strike against Afghanistan in retaliation for Osama bin Laden's al Qaeda destruction of the U.S. embassies in Kenya and Tanzania in 1998: "Our country is committing acts of terrorism according to the definition. What we did is illegal, immoral, inhuman, unacceptable, stupid and un-American."[62]

A few weeks earlier, on October 6, MPAC's Political Advisor Mahdi Bray coordinated and led a rally where approximately 2,000 people congregated in front of the Israeli Embassy in Washington, D.C., to "express their outrage over that country's [Israel's] aggression against Palestinian civilians and holy sites."[63] Hate speeches and exhortations to violence against Jews were heard throughout the rally. "With our blood and soul we will liberate Palestine" was frequently shouted by speakers and the crowd. At one point during the rally, Mahdi Bray played the tambourine as one of the speakers sang, while the crowd repeated: "Al-Aqsa [Mosque] is calling us, let's all go into jihad, and throw stones at the face of the Jews [sic]."

On December 22, 2000, MPAC's Mahdi Bray organized a rally in Lafayette Park outside the White House to celebrate a "Worldwide Day for Jerusalem."[64] In Arabic, the crowd responsively chanted with the emcee, "*Khaybar, Khaybar* oh Jews, the Army of Muhammad is coming for you!" Posters calling for

"Death to Israel" and equating the Star of David with the Nazi swastika were openly displayed and anti-Semitic literature calling for the destruction of the Jews and Israel was distributed. Members of the crowd burned the Israeli flag while marching from the White House to the State Department.

Bray spoke at this rally, along with Imam Mohammed al-Asi, former director of the Islamic Education Center in Potomac, Maryland, who exhorted the crowd to violence in the name of Islam. Al-Asi said: Now, all our *khatibs* (speakers), our imams, our public speakers, should be concentrating on militarizing the Muslim public. This is not a time to make a speaking issue out of this. . . . Muslims have to familiarize themselves with every means possible. . . . Rhetoric is not going to liberate Al-Quds and Al-Aqsa. Only carrying arms will do this task. And it's not going to be someone else who is going to carry arms for you and for me. It is you and me who are going to have to carry these arms.[65]

MPAC's response to a bombing in Jerusalem that killed fifteen, including six children, was telling. On August 9, 2001, a suicide bomber entered a pizza parlor and detonated a bomb that was strapped to his body. A press release by MPAC responded: "[The Jerusalem bombing] is the expected bitter result of the reckless policy of Israeli assassination that did not spare children and political figures. . . . MPAC holds Israel responsible for this pattern of violence."[66]

MPAC also justified Hizballah's 1983 bombing of the American Marine barracks in Beirut as a "military operation" rather than a terrorist attack: "Hezbollah organized the bombing of the Marine barracks in Beirut in October 1983 killing 241 marines, the largest number of American troops killed in a single operation since the end of the Vietnam war. Yet this attack, for all the pain it caused, was not in a strict sense, a terrorist operation. It was a military operation, producing no civilian casualties—exactly the kind of attack that Americans might have lauded had it been directed against Washington's enemies."[67]

In November 1999 Salaam al-Marayati, Executive Director and one of the Founders of MPAC, appeared on "The NewsHour with Jim Lehrer." He responded to accusations that he supports Hizballah. Rather than condemning the terrorist organization, he explained: "If the Lebanese people are resisting Israeli intransigence on Lebanese soil, then that is the right of resistance and they have the right to target Israeli soldiers in this conflict. That is not terrorism. That is a legitimate resistance. That could be called liberation movement, that could be called anything, but it's not terrorism."[68]

THE AMERICAN MUSLIM ALLIANCE (AMA)

The American Muslim Alliance (AMA) was incorporated as a nonprofit organization in California in 1994.[69] According to its articles of incorporation, the AMA was established to raise the political awareness of Muslims in America. Since its establishment the AMA has operated on the state and national levels as a political action committee.

AMA leaders often appear with individuals and institutions that support terrorist organizations. AMA's president, Agha Saeed, has appeared at lectures and events sponsored by Hamas-associated organizations and attended by Hamas supporters. For example, in 1996, 1997, and 1999, Saeed was a guest speaker at the convention of the Islamic Association for Palestine (see Chapter 5). At the 1997 Islamic Association for Palestine Conference held in Chicago, Saeed spoke on several incendiary panels, including one entitled "Zionism: A Racist and Colonialist Ideology."[70] On this panel, Saeed was joined by Sami al-Arian (see Chapter 6).

On June 16, 2000, the AMA's Boston chapter held a fundraiser for Hillary Clinton's Senate campaign. The AMA contributed $50,000 to the campaign. Shortly thereafter, the media began reporting that AMA supported Hamas, culminating in Clinton's returning of all of AMA's campaign contributions. Clinton disagreed with the positions of the AMA, stating, "I have repeatedly supported Israel."[71]

The AMA's president, Agha Saeed, has openly supported armed resistance. At the Islamic Society of North America (ISNA) conference held in Chicago, Illinois, on September 5, 1999, Agha Saeed sanctioned armed resistance against Israel: "United Nations has a resolution . . . which says . . . people in Palestine have the right to resist their oppression by using all means including armed resistance. . . ."

With twenty-five other groups, the AMA co-sponsored a conference in May 1999 in Santa Clara, California, to promote the Islamic State of Palestine in place of the current State of Israel. One speaker, Hatem Bazian, argued, "in the Hadith, the Day of Judgment will never happen until you fight the Jews. They are on the west side of the river, which is the Jordan River, and you're on the east side until the trees and the stones will say, oh Muslim, there is a Jew hiding behind me. Come and kill him! And that's in the Hadith about this, this is a future battle before the Day of Judgment."

The American Muslim Alliance distributed anti-Semitic materials during their Second Annual Conference, held in St. Louis, Missouri, in October of 1997. The organization provided Holocaust revisionist literature to participants. One such article, written by an AMA official, maintained that "the number of Jews killed by Hitler did not exceed one million." Likewise, the article asserted that "there were no execution gas chambers at Auschwitz, Birkenau and Majdanek." In a related vein, the AMA's May-June 2000 Newsletter stated, "Today there are, at most, 5.5 million Jews in the United States. That's just 2 percent of the 275 million residents of the United States. However, by using Holocaust remembrance and support to Israel as catalysts, U.S. Zionists have turned this tiny minority into America's single most influential ethnic lobby, by far!"

On May 24, 1998, the AMA and CAIR sponsored an incendiary rally at Brooklyn College in New York that featured the radical Egyptian cleric Wagdy Ghuneim. Ghuneim argued that "he who equips a warrior of jihad is like the one who makes jihad himself." Ghuneim also led the gathering in a song that included the lyrics, "No to the Jews, descendants of the apes."

The AMA's official mission is to raise public awareness of the religion of Islam and its adherents. Yet its unofficial agenda is clear. Sadly, Islamist extremism has crept into yet another institution of mainstream Muslim society.

ISLAMIC SOCIETY OF NORTH AMERICA (ISNA)

The Islamic Society of North America (ISNA), located in Plainfield, Indiana, and founded in 1981, is the largest Muslim organization in the United States. It serves as an umbrella group for hundreds of Islamic organizations in North America, some of which promote the Islamic fundamentalist doctrines of the Muslim Brotherhood, Hamas, and the Palestinian Islamic Jihad. ISNA publishes a bimonthly magazine, *Islamic Horizons,* which often champions militant Islamist doctrine, and it convenes annual conferences where Islamist militants have been given a platform to incite violence and promote hatred. ISNA is also affiliated with the North American Islamic Trust (NAIT), a nonprofit organization that finances mosques, schools, and community centers across the nation, provides legal advice to Muslim organizations, and advises the Amana Mutual Fund, which invests based on Islamic principles.[72]

The current secretary-general of ISNA is Sayyid Muhammad Syeed. According to the 1988 Articles of Incorporation of Human Concern International, Syeed was one of the original members of that organization's board of directors. One of the primary projects of Human Concern International was to raise funds for the mujahideen in Afghanistan (as well as for Muslims in Africa and Lebanon and for Palestinians in Jordan).[73]

The president of the Board of Directors of ISNA until November 2001 was Muzammil Siddiqui, who also serves as the president of the Islamic Society of Orange County in California. Siddiqui has made statements supporting the violent ideology of radical Islam and shunning the West. In glorifying the jihad in

Afghanistan and its spread to other places in the world, Siddiqui wrote, "I can see there is already some impact of jihad in Afghanistan, in the *intifadah* movement in Palestine . . . *insha'allah,* you will see, in a few years, we will be celebrating, *insha'allah,* the coming victory of Islam in Palestine. . . . We will be celebrating, *insha'allah,* the coming of Jerusalem and the whole land of Palestine, *insha'allah,* and the establishment of the Islamic state throughout that area.[74]

Furthermore, Siddiqui has argued that the "root cause of militant outbreaks in most Muslim countries" is the United States' support of authoritarian regimes.[75] He has also claimed that Islam does not allow a Muslim to fight for non-Muslim causes, such as fighting in the United States Armed Forces. He states, "Islam will not allow a Muslim to be drafted by non-Muslims to defend concepts, ideologies and values other than those of Islam. . . ."[76]

More recently, Siddiqui appeared at a rally in Washington, D.C., where he made statements supporting the outbreak of violence by the Palestinians against the Israelis. Siddiqui's comments contained a decidedly anti-American hue:

> The U.S.A. is directly and indirectly responsible for the plight of the Palestinian people. Our government is responsible for plenty of the injustice that is going on there. The U.S. is the greatest supporter of Israel—economically, militarily, and politically. . . . We want to awaken the conscience of America. America has to learn that. Because if you remain on the side of injus-

tice, the wrath of God will come. Please! Please all Americans, do you remember that, that Allah is watching everyone. God is watching everyone. If you continue doing injustice, and tolerating injustice, the wrath of God will come.[77]

ISNA has assisted in the formation of a number of troubling organizations within the United States. One such was the Holy Land Foundation for Relief and Development (see Chapter 5). Before it was incorporated under the name "The Occupied Land Fund" in 1989, HLF had been a subsidiary of ISNA, using the same mailing address in Plainfield, Indiana.

ISNA's *Islamic Horizons,* which often contains anti-Israel, anti-American, and anti-Semitic sentiments; and which has voiced support for fundamentalism in Sudan, Turkey, and Algeria. The editor is Omer bin Abdullah. ISNA and *Islamic Horizons* have been outspoken in their support for the fundamentalist Islamic regime in Sudan:

> Such activities [conversion to Islam of thousands in Sudan and the use of Sudanese media for *da'wa* purposes] were instituted by the National Salvation Revolution government which took over power in Sudan in 1989. The revolution rid the people of a backward government which was usurping the nation's wealth and draining the military in a losing war in the South. The public trusted the people behind this revolution, who were yesterday's Islamic political prisoners. . . .

Today, Sudan's Popular Arab Islamic Conference, headed by Dr. Hasan Turabi, a Sorbonne-educated lawyer, is shaping to become nothing less than the next United Nations.[78]

In the January/February 1997 edition of *Islamic Horizons*, the United States was attacked as a "big bully" against "Islam, the United Nations and people of color throughout the world":

> Is it an accident that of the four self-proclaimed mortal enemies of America (Libya, Iran, Iraq, and Cuba) three fourths are Muslim countries? . . . Is America the home of a politically powerful, well-organized and financially strong Christian fundamentalist movement whose primary aim is to convert the Muslims throughout the world to Christianity? Is "Israel", the American military-industrial complex, the Christian church, Western multinationals and the Western media united to destroy Islam? . . . Some might well see correlations in their economic crisis with the increased perception of the United States as a big bully—especially regarding Islam, the United Nations and people of color throughout the world.[79]

ISNA's annual conferences are usually held in the Midwest. According to figures reported by ISNA, about 10,000 people participated in its September 1997 conference in Chicago, Illinois. These conferences provide a fund-raising platform for radical Islamic groups. The Islamic Association for Palestine (IAP), the Holy Land Foundation for Relief and Development (HLF), and the Marzook Legal Defense Fund all have substantial ties to Hamas and have been among the groups allowed to participate in an active capacity in ISNA conferences.

These conferences feature speakers ranging from moderate to radical. ISNA has brought in speakers such as Murad Hofmann, a convert to Islam and a former ambassador from Germany to Algeria and Morocco. In the September/October 1997 edition of *Islamic Horizons*, Hofmann denied that both Hamas and the Lebanese Hizballah are terrorist organizations: "Perceptions of 'terrorism' are just as warped when countries considered responsible for harboring, training, and financing 'terrorists' are listed, always several supposedly 'antiwestern' Muslim countries are on the list, as are such movements as Hamas or Hizballah (now synonyms for 'terrorism')."

A BRIEF HISTORY OF ISLAMIC FUNDAMENTALISM

In the wake of September 11, 2001, there has been a great deal of discussion about the "true" nature of Islam and the roots of the militant tradition. What follows is a brief history and analysis which shows that fundamentalism has been a part of Islam from the beginning—but that the modern militant version is a product of the twentieth century.

With Islam there is no separation of church and state. Muhammad himself was a prophet, a warrior, a military general, a lawgiver, and the political head of the Islamic *jama'at* (community). Although many leaders of Muslim countries have tried to establish secular governments, they are constantly exposed to the claim that they are abandoning the true religion.

For this reason, Muslim "fundamentalism" began almost the

day the prophet Muhammad died in 632 c.e. The Prophet had a large family and many followers and the war for succession began almost immediately. This was indeed a "war," characterized wholly by violence, intrigue, and battle. Over the centuries a tradition of peaceful succession among the mullahs—religious leaders—has evolved, just as it has in all other religions. But the melodramatic battle over the true succession of Islam continues even today. Moreover, the extreme purity and austerity of the religious ethos allows an endless parade of reformers to come forth claiming to be the purveyors of the true religion. These "fundamentalists" find continuing support in the poor and dissatisfied masses—although the tiny percentage of fundamentalists who resort to terrorism are often relatively affluent and elite.

It began almost with Muhammad's death. The two main contenders for his position as head of Islam were Abu Bakr, father of Aisha, the Prophet's youngest and favorite wife, and Ali ibn Abi Talib, the Prophet's cousin who was married to his daughter Fatima. During the last week of Muhammad's life, there was much jockeying for position. Abu Bakr had led public prayers during his illness, but Ali had been chosen by the Prophet to wash his body.

Immediately after Muhammad's death, the Muslims of Medina met to choose his successor. Abu Bakr heard of the meeting and rushed to Medina to argue that one of the Prophet's earliest Meccan followers should be the rightful heir. The Medina council agreed and chose Abu Bakr. He died two years later, however, and passed the scepter to Umar ibn Khattab, another Meccan who was the father of Hafsa, another of the Prophet's wives. Ali, a more scholarly man, was disappointed at being passed over again but withdrew to compile an authoritative version of the Koran.

Umar pulled together the Islamic armies and invaded Syria in 638. The following year he advanced to the Euphrates and conquered what is now Iraq and part of Iran. Four years later his armies vanquished Egypt. He set up a system of taxation whereby the Muslim armies were largely supported by revenues raised from the conquered peoples. Within five years of the Prophet's death, Islam controlled most of what is now called the Middle East.

These conquests and all that followed were undertaken under the principle of jihad, or "holy war." The term is used in the Koran and has been interpreted in a number of different ways. In the beginning it did not mean "forced conversion." Rather it meant "the expansion of Islam, by force if necessary." In practice it meant seizing political control, rather than slaughtering unbelievers. Christians and Jews were respected as "people of the book" and were allowed to keep their faith. They were required to pay a sizable tax and many Christians and Jews converted rather than bear the burden. Only pagans were forced to convert or die.

Umar also assumed Muhammad's duties as judge, but here his talents were questionable. He made several highly controversial decisions and Ali began to criticize them in public. Finally Umar ruled against Firuz, an Iranian slave of an Arab master. The slave was so infuriated by the decision that he assassinated Umar in 644. On his deathbed, Umar appointed an electoral college of six elders, including Ali ibn Abi Talib and Uthman ibn Affan, both of whom were married to daughters of the Prophet.

The college offered the caliphate to Ali—but only under the condition that he rule according to the Koran and accept the precedents established by Umar's many decisions. Ali was a man of principle and refused the offer. Uthman was given the same offer and accepted.

Under Uthman, the caliphate degenerated into a cabal of the Meccan clan of the Ummayads, who were the dominant clan before the rise of Muhammad. The Hashimi, who had ascended with Muhammad, were once more in eclipse. Large landholdings in Mesopotamia were handed out to Ummayads and resentment in the provinces grew. In 656 Uthman's house in Medina was besieged by discontented troops from Egypt and Iraq. Two months later, Uthman was murdered. Ali—still highly regarded as the "first of Muslims"—was finally appointed as caliph.

But the Ummayad old guard—particularly Muwaiya ibn Abi Sufian, the governor of Syria, and Aisha, the Prophet's last surviving wife—demanded revenge for Uthman's murder and refused to accept Ali's succession. Aisha raised an army and attacked Ali's forces at Basra but was quickly defeated. Then Muwaiya advanced from Syria with his own army. This time the outcome was not clear-cut. When Muwaiya's forces began to lose, they impaled copies of the Koran on their lances and the fighting ceased. Ali and Muwaiya agreed to arbitration with one representative appointed from each side.

Even before the arbitration began, a faction of Ali's followers rebelled, arguing that arbitration was not in the Koran. Calling themselves the *Kharajis* ("Outsiders"), they also claimed that any Muslim could become caliph—whereas Ali and his main followers wanted to maintain the bloodline through Ali and Fatima. Ali defeated them in battle but enough survived so that they became yet another rebellious faction.

Meanwhile, the arbitration between Ali and Muwaiya also failed. The two parties supposedly agreed to reject both leaders' claims and appoint a third candidate. Ali's arbitrator, being oldest, announced the decision first. But when it came turn for Muwaiya's representative to speak, he reneged on the agreement and declared Muwaiya caliph. This set off a new pandemonium and the two factions remained at war.

In 661 Ali was stabbed to death while at prayer in a mosque by one of the Kharajis. His son Hassan replaced him. By this time the superior social resources of the Ummayad were prevailing, however, and Hassan did not attract many followers. Muwaiya persuaded him to accept a pension and promised that on his own death the caliphate would be returned to Hassan and the Hashimi clan. Hassan was poisoned in 669, however, and once again Muwaiya reneged, appointing his own son Yazid as successor. By the time Muwaiya died in 680, the Ummayads had consolidated their power.

The followers of Ali—now calling themselves the *Shia*—were not through. In 681 Hussein, Ali's oldest son, revived the claim, declaring himself caliph. Dissident factions rallied to his standard, particularly in the city of Kufa in southern Iraq, a rebel stronghold. With his family and an entourage of 40 horsemen and 32 footmen, Hussein began a triumphant procession to meet his supporters in Kufa.

Yazid acted quickly. He dispatched his principal aide, Ubaidullah ibn Ziyad, with an army of 4,000 foot soldiers and cavalry. Ubaidullah quickly quelled dissent in Kufa, then intercepted Hussein's entourage some thirty miles outside the city and demanded his surrender. The ensuing standoff, beginning on the first day of Muharram, the first month of the Islamic year, lasted eight days. Despite being hopelessly outnumbered, Hussein stood firm and refused to surrender his claim. Finally, donning the Prophet's sacred robe, he led his 80 men into battle against 4,000, with martyrdom his reward. One by one his forces were killed, Hussein falling last. His severed head was presented to Yazid.

So ended the first era of dynastic wars among the Muslims. But the matter was not settled. The *Sunna*—"Followers of Tradition"—were triumphant. But the Shia—the "partisans"—maintained their claims that Ali was the true successor and the mullahs his infallible representatives. Shia Islam took root in Persia, while Sunni Islam prevailed in the Arab countries from Egypt to Iraq. Every year Shiites recite the narrative of the "Ten Days of Muharram," recounting Hussein's deliberations and martyrdom. Professional readers recite the story in mosques and meeting halls, accompanied by frenzied wailing and self-flagellation from the congregations. When Shah Reza Pahlavi tried to establish a secular regime in Iran, one of the first things he did was to outlaw this Islamic "passion play." The "Ten Days" has been performed regularly since the rule of the mullahs returned with the Ayatollah Khomeini in 1979.

Even the death of Hussein did not end the conflict. Islam settled down to two separate strains, the Sunni, who represented the Ummayads, the old Meccan aristocracy, and the Shiites, who represented just about everybody else. Muslim suzerainty now spread far and wide, from Spain to Sind, a northwest province of India, with the caliphate at Damascus. As administration grew more complex, Christian bureaucrats from the Byzantine Empire took over. This roused intense resentment among the mullahs. Non-Arabs were also considered second-class citizens—*malawis*—and their resentments mounted. Then there were the descendants of Ali's line, now called *Fatimids*.

In 750 C.E., all these coalesced under Abu Muslim, a former slave, who overthrew the Ummayad dynasty once and for all. In 754 he established a new city at a convergence of the Tigris and Euphrates, Madinat as-Salam, "The City of Peace," more commonly known by its old Persian name, Baghdad. The change was more than geographic. Freed at last from the old Arab aristocracy, Islam finally became a cosmopolitan civilization, a meritocracy that drew its talents from all over the Empire and from all social classes. Reverting to the old Mesopotamian tradition, the caliph became "God's Deputy on Earth," without the need for intercession by the Prophet. The caliph's power was military, but the government was administered by a bureaucracy whose head was the Wazir. As the empire progressed, the army was increasingly composed of specially trained slaves known as Mamluks, mostly of Central Asian Turkic origin. As one Arab historian put it, "This dynast ruled the world with a policy of mingled religion and kingship. The best obeyed by religion while the remainder obeyed from fear." The empire was self-sufficient, growing its food in the fertile Mesopotamian valley and drawing metals from Africa and India. Trade flourished everywhere. Arab coins from the era have been found as far north as Scandinavia. This was the Golden Age of the Arabian Nights.

The caliphate was overextended, however, and broke up quickly. Provinces in Spain and Africa rebelled and became virtually independent. As in Rome, the caliph lost power to his bodyguard and army, who began choosing their own rulers. In 935 a Persian governor conquered the caliph and the rule of Baghdad was over.

A tribal warrior captured Baghdad again in 932 and a kind of division of labor finally evolved. The king exercised political authority while the mullahs maintained spiritual authority. This division created stability but was disapproved by many as contrary to "true Islam." The Shiites mounted a fundamentalist revolt in Tunisia, then moved east, establishing Al Qahira (Cairo) as their palace city. Other schisms occurred. One group of Shiites, the Jaafaris, came to worship Muhammad al-Muntazar (literally, The Awaited Muhammad), who is the infant son of the Eleventh Imam. According to this belief, the Hidden Imam, as he is known, went to sleep in a cave in 873 and will awaken some day to rule Islam. This sect still flourishes in portions of the Middle East today.

The Crusades, which began in 1095, created a huge crisis in the Islamic world. With the loss of Jerusalem in 1187, the caliph at Baghdad suffered a tremendous loss of face. The result was another fundamentalist revival of the Fatimids, who spread their revolt from North Africa across Syria and the Arabian Peninsula. Only Iran and Iraq remained under the caliphate. But this was answered by the rise of Saladin, a Kurdish general who climbed through the ranks and energized the Seljuks, a warlike tribe of Central Asian nomads. These mounted a counterattack on the Fatimids and reconquered most of Islam for Sunni rule. Since then the Shiites have been in decline. Today, they comprise no more than about 15 percent of all Muslims, mostly concentrated in Iran.

Because in Islam the sacred and the secular are one, the battle of "who rules society" is far more intense and is fought as an all-or-nothing affair. Groups such as the Taliban—an organization of religious students who fought for and won political hegemony in Afghanistan—are virtually a constant throughout Islamic history. By contrast, in Western history—in many but not all countries, since the Middle Ages—there are two scepters and the competition for power is alleviated. In Islamic societies, there is only one scepter and the battle is far more intense.

The Wahhab Movement of the eighteenth century, centered on the Arabian Peninsula, revived the idea of pure Islam. Militant Islamic reform emerged once again in the 1920s under the Muslim Brotherhood, founded in Egypt by Hassan al-Banna. Although dedicated to establishing an Islamic state, al-Banna was also moved to reform the inequities of Egyptian society. Over time the Brotherhood has spread throughout the Arab and Muslim world. It became fiercely anti-Western in the 1940s and 1950s under the direction of Sayd Qutb, an Egyptian fundamentalist.

Qutb had a particular animus against the United States. In 1946 he wrote in *Al-Risala*, an Egyptian cultural magazine: "All these Westerners are the same: a rotten conscience, a false civilization. How I hate these Westerners, how I despise all of them without exception." This was not simply the envy of an outsider looking in. In many ways, Qutb felt Muslim civilization was superior. "[The American's] favorite music is Jazz," he wrote in 1951. "This is the kind of music the Negroes invented to satisfy their primitive inclinations . . . it rouses their animal instincts."

Although Egyptian president Gamal Abdel Nasser ruthlessly repressed the Islamic revivalist movement, it developed tentacles throughout the Muslim word, financed largely, even to this day, by wealthy Saudi Arabian and Persian Gulf donors. By the early 1980s, the Iranian Revolution had given it a powerful impetus. The assassination of Egyptian president Anwar Sadat by Muslim extremists at the height of his world power was a strong reminder that even the most esteemed Muslim leaders—be they pro-Western or anti-Western—cannot rest their heads at night without worrying about radical fundamentalists in their own ranks.

Only a few years ago, Libya's Muammar Qaddafi was regarded as the world's most prominent agent of state-sponsored terror. He is still the prime suspect in the downing of Flight 103 in Lockerbie, Scotland. Yet today Qaddafi himself is strangely quiet on the issue of Osama bin Laden and Muslim fundamentalism. The reason is because he himself is now considered "too Western" by fundamentalists and is threatened by radical militants in his own country. In Algeria, tens of thousands have been killed in a struggle between the socialist military dictatorship that holds power and the Islamic Salvation Front, which advocates an Islamic state. Hamas has been active in the Middle East ever since it was founded in 1987, and it quickly spread to the United States.

No country is more central to the American incarnation of Islamic fundamentalism than Afghanistan. In turn, the Muslim leader most responsible for transforming the Afghan jihad into a full-blown international holy war was Sheikh Abdullah Azzam. Killed by a car bomb in Pakistan in 1989 by unknown assailants, he is still regarded reverentially by mujahideen all over the world. On the West Bank, Hamas calls its military wing the Abdullah Azzam Brigades.

Azzam combined hatred for Westerners—Christian, and Jews—with a nostalgia for the days of the Islamic caliphate of centuries long past. "Today humanity is ruled by Jews and Christians—the Americans, the British and others," he told an audience in Kansas in 1988. "Behind them is the fingers of world Jewry, with their wealth, their women and their media. The Israelis have produced a coin on which it is written, 'We shall never allow Islam to be established in the world.' "

Between 1980 and 1989, Azzam and his top aide, Palestinian Sheikh Tamim al-Adnani, visited more than fifty American cities, exhorting their followers to pick up the sword. His Alkhifa Refugee Center opened branches in dozens of these cities, with the help of Osama bin Laden—e.g., the Brooklyn, New York, branch, incorporated in 1987.

In the First Conference of Jihad, held at the Al-Farooq mosque in Brooklyn, Azzam instructed an audience of nearly two hundred to carry out jihad no matter where they were, even in America. "Every Muslim on earth should unsheathe his sword and fight. The word 'jihad' has a special meaning, every time it is mentioned in the Koran. 'Jihad' means fighting of infidels with the sword until they convert to Islam or agree to pay the *jizya* (tribute tax) and be humiliated. The word 'jihad' means fighting only, fighting with the sword."

Notes

Chapter One: How I Made "Jihad in America" and Lived to Tell About It

1. "48 Hours," CBS, April 20, 1995.
2. CNN, April 20, 1995.

Chapter Two: Anatomy of Infiltration

1. Roy Gutman, Daniel Klaidmen, et al., "Bin Laden's Invisible Network," *Newsweek,* October 29, 2001.
2. 60 Federal Register 41152, August 11, 1995.
3. *United States v. One 1997 E35 Ford Van,* United States District Court for the Northern District of Illinois, Case No. 98C-3548, Filed June 8, 1998.
4. *United States v. Usama Bin Laden et al.,* United States District Court for the Southern District of New York, Case No. S(7) 98 Cr. 1023, trial transcript, March 20, 2001.
5. *United States v. Usama Bin Laden et al.,* United States District Court for the Southern District of New York, Case No. S(7) 98 Cr. 1023, trial transcript, February 20, 2001.
6. Donatella Lorch, Daniel Klaidmen, et al., "The Plot Thickens," *Newsweek,* February 7, 2000.
7. *Ibid.*
8. Steve McGonigle, "Airline cuts ties with Holy Land Foundation," *Dallas Morning News,* March 23, 2000; Judith Miller, "US Suspects Charities are Linked to Terrorists," *The Austin American-Statesman,* February 19, 2000.
9. *United States v. Mohammad Youssef Hammoud et al.,* No. 00 CR 147 (W.D. N.C. filed July 20, 2000, amended March 28, 2001), Superseding Bill of Indictment, paragraph 3.

10. "MAYA Condemns Terrorist Attacks," press release, September 11, 2001.

11. "The Mosque in America," A study conducted by the Council on American-Islamic Relations (CAIR) and the Hartford Institute for Religion Research, April 26, 2001.

12. Sheikh Muhammad Hisham Kabbani, "Islamic Extremism: A Viable Threat to U.S. National Security," An open forum at the U.S. State Department, January 7, 1999.

Chapter Three: World Trade Center I

1. El-Sayeed Nosair, "State of Abraham," Notebook captured by authorities in El-Sayeed Nosair's apartment, Cliffside Park, New Jersey. November 5, 1990.

2. Arabic cassette tape captured by authorities in El-Sayeed Nosair's apartment, Cliffside Park, New Jersey, November 5, 1990.

3. Richard Bernstein, "Explosion at the Twin Towers: The Missing Pieces; Convictions in World Trade Center Trial Solve Only Part of a Big, Intricate Puzzle," *The New York Times*, March 5, 1994.

4. "Criminal Practice: Seditious Conspiracy Charge Upheld Against Bombers; U.S., appellee v. Omar Ahmad Ali Abdel Rahman, defendants-appellants; Decided Aug. 16, 1999; Before Newman, Leval, and Parker, C.J.," *New York Law Journal*, August 19, 1999.

5. *Ibid.*

6. Interview with Michael Cherkasky, July 26, 1994.

7. *Ibid.*

8. "Accused World Trade Center bomber lacked cash for bigger bomb: report," Agence France-Presse, October 23, 1997.

9. Benjamin Weiser, "The Trade Center Verdict: The Overview; 'Mastermind' and Driver Found Guilty in 1993 Plot to Blow up Trade Center," *The New York Times*, November 13, 1997.

10. *Ibid.*

Chapter Four: The Source

1. Sardan Tolga, "Bin Laden Contacts, Activities in Turkey Reported," *Instanbul Milliyet* (Internet version), translated from the Turkish, December 7, 1999.

Chapter Five: Hamas

1. This statement was taken from statements given by Hidmi to Israeli authorities after his arrest in Israel in 1993.
2. *Ibid.*
3. Mohammed Salah, quoted in *The New York Times*, February 17, 1993.
4. Bin Yousef's role with the Islamic Association for Palestine is evidenced by numerous volumes of both *The Palestine Monitor* and *Ila Filistin*, the respective English- and Arabic-language periodicals produced by IAP.
5. Ahmed bin Yousef, *Ahmed Yassin: The Phenomenon, the Miracle, and the Legend of the Challenge*, ICRS [Precursor to UASR], 1990.
6. *Ibid.*, p. 56.
7. Ahmed bin Yousef, *Hamas: Background of Its Inception and Horizons of Its March*, ICRS [Precursor to UASR], 2nd ed., September 1989.
8. *Ibid.*
9. *United States v. One 1997 E35 Ford Van*, United States District Court for the Northern District of Illinois, Case No. 98C-3548, Affidavit of Robert Wright, June 8, 1998, para. 53.
10. *In the Matter of the Extradition of Mousa Mohammed Abu Marzook*, United States District Court for the Southern District of New York, Case No. 95 Civ. 9799, Affidavit of Ephraim Rabin, September 28, 1995, paras. 13–14.
11. *In the Matter of the Extradition of Mousa Mohammed Abu Marzook*, United States District Court for the Southern District of New York, Case No. 95 Civ. 9799, Affidavit of Joseph Hummel, October 2, 1995, para. 23.
12. "Group Threatens to Kill Americans," UPI, September 23, 1995.
13. FBI memo by Dale L. Watson, November 5, 2001, "Holy Land

Foundation for Relief and Development/International Emergency Economic Powers Act," p. 15.

14. Ronni Shaked and Aviva Shabi, *Hamas: M'Emunah b'Allah l'Derech ha-Terror (Hamas: From Belief in Allah to the Path of Terror)*, Keter Publishing House, Jerusalem, 1994, p. 171.

15. FBI memo *op. cit.*, p. 31.

16. *Ibid*, p. 45.

17. In a 1994 agreement, the HLFRD "recognized the HLFRD Jerusalem as its sole agency in the West Bank and Israel and authorized it to oversee fund disbursement for programs." FBI memo *op. cit.*, pp. 19–21.

18. Statement by Muhammad Anati to the Israeli authorities, December 17, 1997.

19. FBI memo *op. cit.*, p. 18.

20. *Op. cit.*, p. 19.

21. *Islamic Relief Agency v. The Prime Minister of the State of Israel,* Israeli High Court of Justice, Case No. 3704/96, August 11, 1996.

22. The name of the Hamas commander is unknown; however, his speech, given in Arabic, was recorded on videotape by IAP for future distribution. Annual conference of the Islamic Association for Palestine, Kansas City, Missouri, December 27–30, 1989.

23. "Jihad in America," SAE Productions, aired November 21, 1994.

24. "Announcement of the Information Office of the Islamic Association for Palestine in North America," *Ila Filistin,* November/December 1989, p. 8.

25. Yusuf al-Qaradawi, *The Lawful and the Prohibited in Islam,* International Islamic Federation of Student Organizations, 1992, p. 205.

26. Arabic videotape of the annual conference of the Islamic Association for Palestine, Kansas City, Missouri, December 27–30, 1989.

27. *Ibid.*

28. "Palestine Celebrations," Arabic videotape, Kansas City, Missouri, August 25–26, 1990.

29. Arabic audiotape of the annual conference of the Islamic Association for Palestine, Chicago, December 29, 1996.

30. Audiotape of the annual conference of the Islamic Association for Palestine, Chicago, December 28, 1996.

31. Arabic audiotape of the annual conference of the Islamic Association for Palestine, Chicago, December 26, 1997.

32. Arabic audiotape of the annual conference of the Islamic Association for Palestine, Chicago, December 27, 1997.

33. Arabic audiotape of the annual conference of the Islamic Association for Palestine, Chicago, November 27, 1999.

34. Arabic audiotape of the annual conference of the Islamic Association for Palestine, speech by Imam Jamal Said, Chicago, Illinois, November 24, 2000.

35. Arabic audiotape of the annual conference of the Islamic Association for Palestine, speech by Tariq Suweidan, Chicago, Illinois, November 24, 2000.

36. Arabic audiotape of the annual conference of the Islamic Association for Palestine, speech by unknown speaker, November 24, 2000.

37. "IAP President Statement Regarding Israeli Withdrawal From South Lebanon," posted on IAP's e-mail listserve IAP-Net, May 24, 2000.

38. "Hamas Communiqué Regarding Zionist Attack on Aseera Shamaliya of Nablus," posted on IAP's e-mail listserve IAP-Net, August 28, 2000.

39. *Al-Zaitonah,* June 2, 2000, p. 17.

40. Steve McGonigle, "Local Firm's Accounts Frozen; Investment by wife of Hamas leader is behind decision, lawyer says," *Dallas Morning News,* September 26, 2001.

41. Steve McGonigle, "Firm's export license lifted; Company investigated by terrorism task force predicts exoneration," *Dallas Morning News,* September 8, 2001.

42. Steve McGonigle, "Terrorism task force detains Richardson man; 41-year-old with ties to bin Laden secretary considered a danger to U.S., official says," *Dallas Morning News,* September 23, 2001.

43. *The New York Times,* September 7, 2001.

44. Statements by Muhammad al-Asi, "Jihad in America or Crusade Against Islam," videotape distributed by *Crescent International,* 1995.

45. Statements by Muhammad al-Asi, 23rd annual convention of the Muslim Students Association—Persian Studies Group, Irvine, California, December 25, 1993.

46. *Washington Post,* March 21, 1994.

47. *Washington Post,* August 14, 1994.

48. *The American Spectator,* December 1995.

49. Ahmed Yousef, *The Islamic Movement in the Shadow of International Change and Crisis in the Gulf: The Second Seminar on the Future of Islamic Work,* UASR, 1991, p. 117.

50. *Vision of the Islamic Republic of Iran,* January 31, 1990.

Chapter Six: Jihad in the Academy

1. www.usf.edu/History/histpers.html

2. Ziad abu-Amr, *Islamic Fundamentalism in the West Bank and Gaza,* Indiana University Press, 1994, p. 98.

3. Abu-Amr, p. 99.

4. Articles of Incorporation, Islamic Concern Project Inc., October 20, 1988, Article III.

5. Articles of Incorporation, World and Islam Studies Enterprise (WISE), Inc., February 21, 1991, Article III.

6. Author's interview with Sami al-Arian, August 4, 1994.

7. Proof of the shared addresses and office spaces is evidenced by public record documents issued pursuant to the FBI investigation of ICP and WISE.

8. "A not-so-WISE report at USF," *Tampa Tribune,* May 31, 1996.

9. Interview with Fathi Shikaki, *Inquiry,* January 1993.

10. http://www.qudsway.com.

11. Michael Fechter, "Tampa link to Islamic Jihad uncovered during interview," *Tampa Tribune,* July 28, 1998.

12. Islamic Committee for Palestine Informational Guide.

13. *Al-Liwa,* October 3, 1990, as translated by the Foreign Broadcast Information Service (FBIS) on October 10, 1990. Also see Beverly Milton-Edwards, *Islamic Politics in Palestine,* Tauris Academic Studies, London, 1996, p. 199.

14. Islamic Committee for Palestine Informational Guide.

15. Author's interview with Sami al-Arian, August 4, 1994.

16. ICP rally, Curie High School, Chicago, IL, September 29, 1991.

17. ICP Third Annual Conference, Chicago, IL, December 28–31, 1990.

18. Abu-Amr, p. 90. Ziad abu-Amr is a non-Israeli, non-Western source. He is a respected author and was a professor at Bir Zeit University on the West Bank. His book on Hamas and the Islamic Jihad was originally published in Arabic in 1989 under the title *Al-Harakah Al-Islamiah fi Al-Diffah Al-Gharbiyeh wa Kittah Ghaza (The Islamic Movement in the West Bank and Gaza Strip)*. This book was translated into English and republished in 1994 under the title *Islamic Fundamentalism in the West Bank and Gaza*. Abu-Amr is currently a member of the Palestinian National Council. Abu-Amr had first-hand knowledge of the WISE–PIJ combination because he attended a joint conference of WISE and USF on December 5, 1991. See William Reece Smith, Jr., Report of his findings to the University of South Florida, p. 72, and Shallah's resume.

19. Abu-Amr, p. 117–118.

20. Meir Hatina, *Islam and Salvation in Palestine* (Moshe Dayan Center for Middle Eastern and African Studies, 2001), pp. 24–7, 29, 31, 40, 42, 98, 104.

21. Abu-Amr, pp. 94–95.

22. Resume of Ramadan Abdullah Shallah.

23. In a book published in 1990, Thomas Mayer wrote that Fathi Shikaki had met Bashir Nafi in Egypt and developed a relationship with him in Gaza. According to Mayer, Shikaki found Nafi to be an "ideological friend." Mayer also pointed out that Nafi, while in Egypt, had "given refuge to a suspect in Sadat's assassination." See Thomas Mayer, "Pro-Iranian Fundamentalism in Gaza," in Emmanuel Sivan and Menachem Friedman, eds., *Religious Radicalism and Politics in the Middle East*, State University of New York Press, Albany, 1990, p. 148; see also Aviva Shabi and Ronni Shaked, *Hamas: M'Emunah B'Allah L'Derech Ha-Terror (Hamas: From Belief in Allah to Terror)*, Keter Publishing House, Jerusalem, 1994, pp. 207, 210–211.

24. Ramadan Shallah lists on his resume that he was on the editorial board of the publication *Al Alam* out of London from 1987 to 1989, and Bashir Nafi's resume shows that he was on the same board from 1985 to 1987.

25. In Shabi Aviva's book *Hamas*, co-authored with Ronni Shaked, a for-

mer officer in the Israeli General Security Services (the Israeli equivalent of the FBI), the PIJ London activities involving Shallah and Nafi are described:

Moreover, he [Shikaki] had founded a front based in London to ensure easier communication with the Occupied Territories. . . . The main channel of communication between the headquarters in Damascus to the activists in the territories was through the London base of the movement. All activities in London were directed by Dr. Ramadan Shallah, who was born in Gaza. Shallah was one of the first Islamic Jihad members in the territories and was among the people who were most close to Dr. Shikaki.

He went to England to continue his studies and was appointed as the head of the London branch. At the end of 1988, he arrived to London, as well as Bashir Nafi from the Kalandia Refugee Camp. After his deportation from the territories, Nafi was sent to assist Dr. Shallah.

From their base in London, they both ran the activities of Islamic Jihad in the territories—the military activity, the information, the advertising, and the distribution of the communiques. The base in London was responsible for delivering the money to finance the activity and for sending the Islamic Jihad communiques which were distributed throughout the Occupied Territories. The contact man in Gaza was Omar Shallah, who was Dr. Ramadan Shallah's younger brother, and was a member in one of the PIJ units.

Since they were afraid of someone listening, the Islamic Jihad people used a very sophisticated method of communication: Dr. Ramadan would call his brother from London using codewords which by then Omar meant would have to wait until night for the next operational orders. The base for communication was an industrial business in the center of Israel from which Omar's friend used to work, where he could call London and talk for hours with no disturbances. During these conversations, Nafi used to dictate to Omar the context of the next fliers and to tell him about the next military instructions or to guide him in other issues concerning the movement. The text of the fliers and the instructions were sent by Ramadan Shallah to Dr. Jamil Alyan who was responsible for the distribution of the fliers in the territories. (pp. 207, 210–211)

26. According to an article in the *Jerusalem Post*, from 1986 until 1991 Shallah lived in England where he was "the contact man between Jihad operatives in Europe and the territories. Together with Bashir Nafa [*sic*], Shalah [*sic*] headed the organization's British office, which funneled money to the territories. He also drafted most of the leaflets the group distributed in the territories." "New Jihad Head was Active in Britain, US," *Jerusalem Post*, October 31, 1995.

27. Ramadan Shallah lists on his resume "A Founding Member of . . . the World & Islam Studies Enterprise WISE (1990) (London U.K. & Tampa)" and "Member of the Editorial Board of *Qira 'at Siyasiyyah (Arabic Quarterly),* Managing Editor, Tampa, 1991–Present." Bashir Nafi also notes on his resume that he was on the editorial board of WISE's journal *Qira 'at Siyasiyyah* in 1990 and attended Islamic Committee for Palestine conferences in 1988 and 1989.

28. See, for example, Mayer, "Pro-Iranian Fundamentalism."

29. "Islamic terrorism: Tehran to Tampa," *New York Post*, November 14, 1995.

30. "A not-so WISE report at USF," *Tampa Tribune*, May 31, 1996.

31. Affidavit of William West, INS Supervisory Special Agent, November 17, 1995.

32. Affidavit of Barry Carmody, FBI Special Agent, December 19, 1995.

33. This letter was released in August 2000 as an exhibit in the immigration bond hearings of Dr. Mazen al-Najjar.

34. This translation was provided by the INS as a supplement to the letter, originally written in Arabic.

35. *In the Matter of Mazen al-Najjar,* Case No. A26-599-077, Custody Redetermination Proceedings, Testimony of William West, INS Supervisory Special Agent, July 18, 1996.

36. "Behind al-Arian's façade," *St. Petersburg Times*, November 1, 2001.

Chapter Seven: Osama bin Laden, Sheikh Abdullah Azzam, and the Birth of al Qaeda

1. Arabic videotape of the First Conference of Jihad, Al-Farook Mosque, Brooklyn, New York, 1988.
2. Arabic videotape of the annual conference of the Muslim Arab Youth Association (MAYA), Oklahoma City, Oklahoma, December 1988.
3. *Ibid.*
4. *Atlantic Monthly,* November 1994.
5. Reuters Financial Service, September 13, 1993.
6. *Al-Quds al-Arabi,* Feb. 7, 1997.
7. *United States v. Siddig Ali et al.,* United States District Court for the Southern District of New York, Case No. S(3) 93 Cr. 181, Government Exhibit 307-T, May 16, 1993, received into evidence May 25, 1995.
8. Translation posted onto the MSANews Web site by the Committee for the Defense of Legitimate Rights (CDLR), October 12, 1996 (http://msanews.mynet.net//MSANEWS/199610/19961012.3.html).
9. "Get Ready for Twenty World Trade Center Bombings," *The Middle East Quarterly,* June, 1997.
10. *United States v. Usama Bin Ladin et al.,* United States District Court for the Southern District of New York, Case No. S(5) 98 Cr. 1023, Indictment, May 19, 1999, para. 10(b).
11. *United States v. Abu Doha,* United States District Court for the Southern District of New York, Case No. 01 Mag. 1242, Complaint, para. 1.
12. *Ibid.*
13. *Ibid.*
14. *Ibid.*
15. *Ibid.*
16. James Gordon Meek, "American Terror Suspect Charged in Jordan: New Revelations About Activities in the U.S.," APBNews.com, January 19, 2000.
17. *United States v. Ali Mohamed,* United States District Court for the Southern District of New York, Case No. S(7) 98 Cr. 1023, Plea of Ali Mohamed, October 20, 2000.

18. *Jane's Intelligence Review,* December 1, 1998.
19. *International Herald Tribune,* January 21, 1999.
20. *U.S. News & World Report,* May 15, 1995.

Chapter Eight: Fighting Back

1. Teresa Watanabe, "A Holy War of Words in Islamic U.S.," *Los Angeles Times,* April 15, 1999.
2. Sheik Muhammad Hisham Kabbani, "Islamic Extremism: A Viable Threat to U.S. National Security," An open forum at the U.S. State Department, January 7, 1999.
3. *Ibid.*
4. *Ibid.*
5. *Ibid.*
6. *Ibid.*
7. Sam Grewal, "Muslims Face Hostility Within," *Toronto Star,* October 13, 2001.
8. Seif Ashmawy, Hearing of Senate Foreign Relations Committee, Near East and South Asia Subcommittee, March 19, 1996.
9. *Ibid.*
10. Editor for Cultural Affairs, "The Author, Khalid Duran, is an Apostate—Muslims of America Declare Him a Non-Believer," *Ash-Shahid,* Amman, May 2001.
11. Iviews.com, "Jewish Group Criticized for Phony Fatwa," July 4, 2001.
12. See "The Story of the Forged Fatwa," *Az-Zaituna,* July 20, 2001.
13. See AP, "Jordanian Muslim Group Denies Threat," July 22, 2001.
14. See 'Ala AbuDallu, "AbuZant: 'Yes, Khalid Duran is an Apostate, shedding his blood is permissible'," *Ash-Shahid,* July 22, 2001.
15. "Peace Offering Opens New Wounds," *Washington Post,* July 1, 2001.

Appendix C: The Terrorists' Support Networks

1. "On Whom Money Should be Spent," *Friday Report,* January–February 1995.
2. Arabic videotape from the annual conference of the Muslim Arab Youth Association (MAYA), Oklahoma City, December 23–28, 1992.

3. *Ibid.*

4. Arabic videotape from the annual conference of the Muslim Arab Youth Association (MAYA), Chicago, December 24, 1994.

5. *Ibid.*

6. Arabic audiotape from the annual conference of the Muslim Arab Youth Association (MAYA), Ontario, California, December 29, 1997.

7. *Islam Report,* April/May 1994.

8. *Ibid.*

9. This information was taken from the "World of Islam Resource Guide" on the MSANews Web site at http://msanews.mynet.net. Two years earlier, in a December 1994 article entitled "Algeria, the Crown Jewel of Islamic Revival," the *Islam Report* celebrated that "Thousands of Army, Police and naval officers and soldiers joined *Mujahideen* against the un-Islamic regime . . . Towns and cities [*sic*] residents are giving every possible aid they can afford to Jihad, while regime forces are retreating everyday."

10. *Islam Report* on MSA News, "Al-Qital Newsletter," May 12, 1996.

11. *Islam Report,* March 1995.

12. *AIG Email,* April 1996.

13. Vernon Loeb, "A Global, Pan-Islamic Network; Terrorism Entrepreneur Unifies Groups Financially, Politically," *The Washington Post,* August 23, 1998.

14. *Agence France-Presse,* June 16, 1996. CDLR also declared that the 500,000 Shi'a Muslims in Saudi Arabia were apostates. This was an extremely serious charge, as apostasy in Saudi Arabia is punishable by death; *New York Times,* May 14, 1993.

15. This address change is verified through the Lexis-Nexis Finder software.

16. *Washington Post,* October 9, 1999.

17. Hizb-ut-Tahrir Web site, 1998.

18. The Islamic State, operating under the caliphate system, was implemented following the death of Muhammad in the early 7th century, and continued, uninterrupted, through the destruction of the Ottoman Empire in the 1920s.

19. Hizb-ut-Tahrir Web site, 1998.

20. *Ibid.*

21. A saying of the Prophet Muhammad, quoted on the Hizb-ut-Tahrir Web site.

22. Hizb-ut-Tahrir Web site, 1998.

23. Taqiuddin an-Nabhani, *Islamic Concepts,* produced by Al Khilafah, UK.

24. Hizb-ut-Tahrir considers King Hussein and the Hashemite Clan to be "Kufr," or infidels.

25. Hizb-ut-Tahrir, *The Plan to Eradicate Islam in the Middle East.*

26. "Entering the Society," *Khalif'ornia Journal,* January–June 1997.

27. *Khalif'ornia,* July/August 1992.

28. *Khalif'ornia,* December 1995.

29. "Qaid'a: A Legal Principle," *Khalif'ornia Journal,* January–March 1996.

30. "Treaties in Islam," *Khalif'ornia Journal,* April–June 1996.

31. "Islam, Politics and History," *Khalif'ornia Journal,* April–June 1996.

32. Nihad Awad, "Muslim-Americans in Mainstream America," *The Link,* February–March 2000.

33. Arabic audiotape from the Brooklyn College rally, May 24, 1998.

34. "CAIR demands removal of billboard stereotyping Muslims," CAIR-Southern California Action Alert, October 28, 1998.

35. *Ibid.*

36. Ibrahim Hooper, "Media and You," panel discussion at CAIR's "Leadership Ambassadors, Making a Difference" conference in Columbus, Ohio, June 9, 2001.

37. Statement by Nihad Awad at a panel discussion, "The Road to Peace: The Challenge of the Middle East," Barry University, March 22, 1994.

38. Statement by Nihad Awad, Al-Awda rally in Lafayette Park, Washington, D.C., September 16, 2000.

39. *Ibid.*

40. CNN "Crossfire," November 18, 1999.

41. English audiotape from the annual conference of the Islamic Association for Palestine (IAP), Chicago, November 25, 1999.

42. Jeff Jacoby, "Muslim silence about Islamic crimes," *Boston Globe,* June 24, 1999.

43. *Muslim World Monitor,* March 10, 1994.

44. AMC 1995 IRS Form 990.

45. *AMC Report*, April 1995.

46. "Problems at American Muslim Council (AMC)," *Pakistan Link*, May 12, 2000.

47. AMC Web site, October 10, 1997.

48. *Paris Radio Monte Carlo*, December 9, 1995.

49. "A bank account has been opened in the Arab Bank, Shimsani Branch, Amman, in the names of Najib Rashdan and Layth Shubaylat . . . so that support may be given from those who are in solidarity with Ahmad [Daqamisa]," *Al-Zaytona*, #139, April 11, 1997.

50. *Palestine Times*, September 1999.

51. Michael Lewis, "The Washington Report on Middle East Affairs," *Near East Report*, May 11, 1992.

52. The statements by Alamoudi were recorded on videotape by an individual participating in the rally.

53. U.S. State Department daily press briefing, February 13, 2001. Proof of Alamoudi's participation in the conference was provided in the form of a photograph of Alamoudi with two other American individuals, Yasser Bushnaq and Imad ad-Deen Ahmad at http://www.minaret.org/beirutconference.htm.

54. "Conference backs Palestinian uprising, calls for strategy to eliminate Israel," Associated Press, January 31, 2001.

55. *Iqamat al-Din:* establishment of the Islamic system in both personal and collective life.

56. *An Introduction to ICNA* (pamphlet), revised 1987.

57. Abdul Malik Mujahid, president, Islamic Circle of North America (ICNA), in response to a question from the audience. Videotape of the annual conference of the Islamic Society of North America (ISNA), Columbus, Ohio, September 1995.

58. ICNA representative Sayid Thaqib. Videotape of the annual conference of the Islamic Association for Palestine (IAP), Kansas City, December 1989.

59. English audiotape of the annual convention of the Islamic Circle of North America, Baltimore, Maryland, June 30, 2000.

60. MPAC Web site, http://www.mpac.org/about/about_menu.shtml.

61. Maher Hathout, "Washington D.C. Rally in Prospective," *The American Muslim,* Vol. 2, No. 1, January 2001.

62. Maher Hathout, "An Immoral Response," Friday sermon at the Islamic Center of Southern California (ICSC), August 21, 1998, posted on the *Voice of Islam* Web site.

63. "Subject: CAIR-NET: D.C.-Area Mosques Rally for Jerusalem/Gore Supporters Use Slurs against Muslims," Posted by CAIR on http:msanews.mynet.net, October 5, 2000. Bray is listed as the coordinator.

64. "Subject: AMC-NET: December 22 Rally for Jerusalem in Washington, D.C.," Posted by the American Muslim Council on http:msanews.mynet.net, December 18, 2000.

65. These quotes were transcribed from a videotape of the rally.

66. MPAC Press Release, "MPAC Issues Statement on August 8 Bombing in Jerusalem," August 9, 2001.

67. Salaam al-Marayati, "A Position Paper on U.S. Counterterrorism Policy," Multi Media Vera International, June 1999.

68. Salaam al-Marayati, "Muslims in America," "NewsHour" with Jim Lehrer, November 24, 1999.

69. Articles of Incorporation, August 19, 1994.

70. December 27, 1997, 11:00-12:30 PM, Hyatt Regency Hotel, Chicago, IL.

71. "Hillary Clinton to Return Muslim Donations," United Press International, October 26, 2000.

72. According to the Web site of NAIT (http://www.nait.net), it serves the following purposes:

    NAIT provides protection and safeguarding for the assets of ISNA/MSA [Muslim Students Association] and other communities by holding their assets and real estate in waqf. It also initiates and manages profitable business ventures in accordance with the Islamic Shari'ah; supports and subsidizes projects beneficial to the cause of Islam and Muslims.

73. "The Role of the Islamic Associations in the Afghani war," *Al-Jihad,* December 1986, p. 27.

74. Muzammil Siddiqui, "The Establishment of the Islamic Government in Afghanistan," date unknown.

75. "Media officials get lesson in reporting on Islam without stereotyping," *The Minaret*, May/June 1993.

76. "Basic Principles of Involvement in War in Islam," *The Message International*, February 1991.

77. Statements by Muzammil Siddiqui, Jerusalem Day Rally, Washington, D.C., October 28, 2000.

78. *Islamic Horizons*, March/April 1996, p. 26.

79. *Islamic Horizons*, January/February 1997, p. 29–30.

Index